# Responsible Management

# Responsible Management

## *Understanding Human Nature, Ethics, and Sustainability*

Kemi Ogunyemi

First published in 2013 by
Business Expert Press, LLC
222 East 46th Street, New York, NY 10017
www.businessexpertpress.com

ISBN-13: 978-1-60649-504-9 (paperback)

ISBN-13: 978-1-60649-505-6 (e-book)

DOI 10.4128/9781606495056

Business Expert Press Principles for Responsible Management Education collection

Collection ISSN (print): Forthcoming
Collection ISSN (electronic): Forthcoming

Cover design by Jonathan Pennell
Interior design by Exeter Premedia Services Private Ltd., Chennai, India

First edition: 2013

10 9 8 7 6 5 4 3 2 1

Printed in the United States of America.

*To my parents, with gratitude and love*

# Abstract

This book serves as a valuable complementary text for courses on Ethics, Responsibility, Leadership, Corporate Social Responsibility, and Sustainability, which mostly tend to neglect their human nature dimensions. It provides an understanding of human nature and its uniqueness and complexity, which helps managers in today's business world to better manage and to respect self, others, and the environment. It also provides the foundation for learning ethical behavior, leadership, responsibility, sustainable management, and corporate social responsibility. Without this angle, an MBA might tend to focus primarily on financial success in different dimensions—operational quality, financial strategy, workforce motivation, cost-cutting strategies, etc. and people may forget to take cognizance of the implications of their own nature and that of the people through whom they have to work. Future leaders and shapers of sustainable organizations and societies cannot afford to have such a knowledge gap. Having these discussions helps students understand that the reason to be ethical goes beyond self-interest and profit motives to the very foundations of human nature.

The cases and principles discussed in this book are focused towards postgraduate business courses but are easily adaptable to all levels and spheres of education since the concepts can be applied universally. The book is designed as a simple and thought-provoking resource to prepare students to relate better with themselves and with other people. While providing useful insights for everyone, it is particularly helpful for those who have to work with others or lead them, whether formally or informally.

*Responsible Management: Understanding Human Nature, Ethics, and Sustainability* offers a detailed discussion of the basic characteristics or features of the nature of human beings, using short cases and scenarios of real workplace situations to explain them. It also suggests the way to teach some of these principles in a practical way in class, through experiential learning methods. The cases provide rich experiences that help students to connect to the topics in a practical and relevant manner.

Some of the learning methods are embedded in the text itself as exercises and projects while others are made available to faculty through the website of the publishers. The book fits into Area 1, educator guides, of the Principles for Responsible Management Education (PRME) Collection, as a textbook for the course, and aims to provide a focus on responsible personhood that directly feeds into the six PRME principles, especially principles 1 and 3.

*Principle 1 states: We will develop the capabilities of students to be future generators of sustainable value for business and society at large and to work for an inclusive and sustainable global economy.* Responsible Management: Understanding Human Nature, Ethics, and Sustainability explains to students the need to understand, appreciate and value human life and to offer business and society valid value propositions that are truly beneficial to mankind and to the world we live in.

*Principle 3 states: We will create educational frameworks, materials, processes, and environments that enable effective learning experiences for responsible leadership.* By deepening their understanding of human nature, *Responsible Management: Understanding Human Nature, Ethics, and Sustainability* helps students to more easily assimilate the principles that underlie ethical decision-making and responsible and accountable leadership. They develop a heightened sensitivity to others' needs and are thus enabled to start acting habitually on motives other than self-interest. The increase in their level of self-reflection and self-control that comes from knowing human nature better is also a great help in achieving the necessary qualities for self-leadership and for leading others.

Each chapter contains a real managerial scenario presented as a mini case study, a discussion of selected human characteristics with workplace situational examples and illustrations, and suggested exercise(s) or project(s).

There are more and more business schools teaching courses in Ethics, Leadership, Corporate Social Responsibility, Sustainability, and Responsible Management. For these courses, understanding human nature and behavior is a fundamental need. Thus, the book can serve as new and complementary material to the already existing books for these courses and as support material to Organizational Behavior courses.

This book tries to provide practical knowledge and life skills, as is evidenced in the testimonies from MBAs who attended the course—titled "The Nature of Human Beings"—in 12 to 15 sessions at the beginning of their MBA program. It is also useful for non-business schools who will wish their graduates to be well grounded in concepts of professional ethics and responsibility. In addition, practitioners who wish to enhance their practice of management will benefit from reading it.

## Keywords

abstraction and reflection, anthropology, behavioral ethics, business, business and society, career success, case study, character building, commitment, communication, corporate social responsibility, development, diversity, emotion, ethics, experiential learning, freedom, fulfillment, human nature, human resource management, intellect, leadership, locus of control, management, managing people, organizational behavior, PRME, respect, responsibility, sustainability, values, virtue, will, work, workplace situations

# Contents

x   CONTENTS

# Acknowledgment

I am grateful to my family for their love and support.

I would like to thank Imelda Wallace, Margaret Isebor, Salem Al Ismaily, and Fr. John Paul Taberner for their invaluable help in going through the book in its drafting stages and making suggestions for its improvement. Special thanks go to Juan Manuel Elegido for the patience and wisdom that shone through his comments after reviewing the first draft and for all the helpful materials with which he provided me.

I would also like to thank Oliver Laasch for his help and direction with this project.

Last but not least, I thank David Parker, Cindy Durand, Sheri Dean, and Denver Harris, of Business Expert Press and Exeter Premedia, for their encouragement and cooperation in the process of getting this work done.

I also wish to express sincere appreciation to my friends and students in MBA 8, 9, 10, and 11 for the many discussions we have had about the nature of human beings and for their generous and unreserved readiness to share their stories.

# Testimonies

## Emmanuel Ikehi

This course has influenced my life immensely. If a course like this was introduced into the curriculum in schools, I do believe Nigeria would have a brighter future. I now know that there were some people whom I unconsciously classified as lesser human beings, like *okada*[1] riders, because of their behavior. This was mainly based on hasty generalization; I never really saw them as human beings because of the way they act, but now I've realized that every human being is unique, no matter the way they are or what they do and so they should be treated as such. Also educating my emotions is very key because I am more of a feeling person; I am trying to balance this and use it to advantage.

Generally, this course has made clear to me the things I need to acquire and their importance (virtues, values) and the things I need to balance (uniqueness of man, emotions), in order to be able to manage people effectively. Also, I had always felt the carrot-and-stick approach was the best way to get people to work effectively but now I know that human beings are different; what works for one person might not necessarily work for another.

I already know I am becoming a better person. In terms of my personal and career choices I have a clearer understanding of the areas I need to work on. Some of these areas are people motivation in order to get the best from them and establishing better superior–subordinate relationships. I plan to use these to make myself a better manager in my workplace, in my home and generally in all aspects of my life. In every aspect of life I have a choice and I have made the choice to make choices based on reason and benefit, to improve both myself and others around me.

---

[1] Colloquial name for commercial public transportation bikes in Nigeria

In terms of career choices, I will be more specific in my choice of a place of work, taking into account their value stance and its implementation, how they see their staff and what is most important to them.

Also in the future, when I establish my own company, I intend to build a very strong nonnegotiable foundation based on values that are beneficial to each staff as a person. I believe this is the key to success and to the kind of loyalty from one's employees that one will need to make one's company achieve and surpass its set targets or goals.

## Chibuzo Okechukwu-Ode

This course has enabled me to see human beings differently. Every human being is different. I now consider people as individuals with their own temperament and personality. That they have these tendencies does not make them bad. An example is my husband who likes social gatherings while I prefer to stay at home with my family.

I also now see people as having intelligence and will. They are able to reason on their own though their reasoning may be different from mine; but that is what makes us human beings. I now try to be more accommodating of people's ideas because they will not always think like me.

Apart from using our reasoning, I have also come to realize that as human beings we have certain senses, instincts and emotions we share with animals. This is existent in all humans and sometimes we exhibit these traits. I am trying to educate my emotions especially when it comes to anger. This has brought greater peace in my house because I have actually reduced the way I shout. I am also currently working well with my team members at school. I have also learnt that emotions are innate in human beings. When someone exhibits the wrong emotions I should not react to it by exhibiting my own emotions immediately without making use of my intellectual cognition and appetition.

I have determined to educate many of my emotions so as to turn out a better person. One of such emotions which I am determined to educate is anger. I am also determined to develop a good character. With all these my life is on the path to change; the important thing being that I have reasoned and thought out certain attributes or temperaments I need to work on in myself and I am emotionally disposed and determined to achieve this.

As I mentioned earlier, I have reevaluated my past life, especially my behavior and character in my personal life and career. I have also determined certain areas I need to work on. Such areas include anger, aggressiveness, and being argumentative. I believe that, in future, based on the fact that I have learnt a lot about human beings, I will handle people differently both at home and at work. For example, I used to shout a lot and whenever I shouted I seemed to achieve results which always ended up being short-lived. Reasoning with people that I work with or come in contact with will achieve longer-term results.

In my personal life, I have realized that each human being is born with a temperament that is exclusive to him or her. This means that my children will not behave exactly the way I behave or the way their father behaves. The implication of this is that as they grow up, I should not always expect them to like or dislike the things I like or dislike. They will be given a certain liberty to make their career choices depending on where they feel they will fit in.

For my career choice, I have decided that after my MBA I will attach more weight to the intrinsic goods that I can get from a workplace than the extrinsic goods they have to offer. I will search for a career bearing in mind how they treat their staff and not just how much they pay. Careerwise I will try not to manipulate individuals but rather appeal to their reasoning ability. I will also treat my co-workers with dignity and allow my subordinates contribute to issues.

## Chiamaka Obike

The first thing that I learnt in "Nature of Human Beings" is that it is dangerous to make assumptions because the truth is always outside us. I learnt that we do not only need to ask questions but we need to ask the right questions. To ask the right question, we need to have some facts of the case. I have realized that my house help, whom I assumed was callous and careless, was actually naïve. I now teach her a lot of things which I assumed she knew. I have learnt better ways to give instructions and ask questions to appeal to her intelligence so that I can get the results I need.

I was also exposed to the fact that every human being has the power of free choice. There are two terms there: "free" and "choice." Freedom is when one has alternatives to choose from and choice is when one decides to take a course of action as against another. And whatever action one decides to do has consequences or, better put, entails commitments.

This was very scary to me because one may not know the details of the commitments involved as at the time of decision. But it is good to know that I can choose my own commitment rather than being dragged into it. I can decide to be proactive by making choices and setting goals for my life rather than leaving things to chance.

Now, I make choices knowing that not making a choice is a choice in itself. I am no longer scared of commitments that come from my choice because it is in those commitments that my freedom becomes effective.

One of the recent choices I've made is to accept one of my relatives though she is going to constrain me in some ways, but within her constraints I will really be free to relate with her and harness all her good qualities.

Another thing which I learnt and which helps me now is that virtues are not natural to any man. Everyone who has one virtue or the other (integrity, justice, temperance, etc.) had at one time or the other desired and developed it. I am working towards developing some virtues by practicing them. I am happy to realize that those who I thought naturally had some virtue, had times when they struggled to acquire it, and so I am not the only one who is striving towards shaping myself through the development of virtues.

Regarding my career choice, I now understand myself better and know what fulfils me. Based on that, I can make choices to establish a direction for my career. In decision-making, because I have been equipped with the knowledge of human nature, I will treat everyone (my co-workers, domestic staff, etc.) with respect. I also know that monetary compensation alone will not fulfill me; the defining factor for employment will be what I am happy doing as well as a good pay.

As a manager, I think I can make better judgments and good decisions as I now have a better understanding of human nature. Now I know that human beings are not donkeys who are motivated merely by carrots and sticks but that they are motivated to act when they see the reason to. In my home, I hope to be a good manager of the resources and of the people living with me.

# Busola Fadehan

So far, the course has influenced my life by enhancing my knowledge of human behavior which is obviously a good foundation on which to base a whole career (as a manager) of managing human beings. The course has also increased my understanding of the impact of emotions, intelligence and freedom of choice on human nature, which makes us quite distinctive animals.

I have also learnt from the course how to attain true fulfillment in life which should not be limited to myself and my interests but should indeed focus on creating value for other people that I work with and come in contact with.

The course on the nature of human beings has touched me greatly by making me realize that the differences such as intelligence, productivity, temperament, personality and so on in other people all around me are fundamental and should be respected. This means listening to other people's opinion, involving them in making decisions and communicating to them their true worth as human beings.

The course will help me in managing my interpersonal relationships with other people better. By being more conscious of the impact of emotions on my behavior towards others I hope to be able to practice to be more accommodating with people and get beyond normal prejudices, such as ethnicity and religion, which may affect my being able to achieve positive relationships with other people. I will be able to achieve this through educating my emotions constantly.

The course will also help me to respect and appreciate other people's freedom of choice as regards making certain key decisions.

Professionally and careerwise, the course will help me in the future as a manager to be able to seek the right forms of motivation for my subordinates by making them see the point and get the "big idea" in doing certain things rather than make assumptions using the carrot and stick approach. It will also enhance my appreciation for my employees so that I treat them as persons rather than use them as economic tools in business.

Also as a manager, it will help me to strive for mutuality in business relations so that in making certain key decisions in the organization I will put the true interests of all the parties into consideration and ensure that nobody is treated as a pure instrument for the interests of the organization.

As a prospective manager the course will help me to resort to legitimate persuasion as a means of achieving objectives rather than to using manipulative ways to try and change employees' natural inclinations and preferences without counting on their power of choice. Thus, I will be making them more committed to serve.

## Akin Akinwunmi

1. I am now conscious of my own emotions and I am learning to control them by trying to create a balance between the different types of emotions. Also, I have started reading emotions in others and responding appropriately to them.

2. Since man has the power to choose, I now choose what to think, imagine and do, and by so doing I am educating my emotions.

3. In expressing my freedom, I now think of its consequences to other people in my environment so that it won't spark conflicts.

4. In order to encourage people to do something, I try to help the person experience the appropriate emotions as this is more effective.

5. I always keep in mind that I have to learn from the views of others and always have to be open to criticism.

6. Rather than try to manipulate people, I am learning to persuade them by giving them a reason and allowing them to choose.

7. I now know that extrinsic goods are important but they only make sense as means to get intrinsic goods. Humans cannot get fulfillment by acquiring extrinsic goods alone. What I will focus on is how I can use my extrinsic good to get intrinsic good.

8. I will be a better person because I know it is possible to educate my intellect and will.

9. In looking for a job, I won't limit my attention to considerations of pay and career prospects but will also to try to identify an organization with whose objectives I can identify and which takes serious interest in employees.

10. Rather than adopt the concept of carrot and sticks in relating with people (children, staff, etc.), I now prefer to help them experience the

appropriate emotions as this is more effective in achieving a lasting behavior change.

11. Since I know all humans are unique in their own way, studying the nature of human beings will make me appreciate people better and also respect their freedom. Every man has a right to choose his destiny.

It is only by being aware of and grateful for our power to choose that we can take our destiny in our hands and set out to do something specific to create a better future for ourselves. I can choose to base my business on principles and values.

## Akinola Oladejo

Before beginning this course, I thought I had a good grasp of the nature of human beings since I have been relating with a lot of different human beings all my life.

However, below are some of the major areas in which the course has influenced my life.

**Perception of all human beings**: I now have a broader perspective on what a man is composed of and this helps me to know why some people behave the way they do. No human being is perfect.

**Man's dignity**: Basically, this topic has been most impactful to me. The understanding that all men are equal has given me a new orientation as to how to relate with all people around me no matter their status or relationship with me. I give everybody the respect I should give to every human being regardless of what I am expecting from them.

I now know that when I am using people only for what I can get from them, I only manipulate them. In the end I would not maximize the productivity I could have got from them if they saw the point of doing what they do.

**Man's freedom**: This has opened my eyes to so many realities of life that I didn't know or didn't take seriously. For example, based on my freedom of choice (that I now understand better) I took a decision which I should have taken a long time ago. The understanding that my reluctance to make a decision actually limits me is what made me make a decision. And since taking that decision, I have moved on and lived a happier life.

Also, I have been used to dwelling on my constraints, fighting for my *freedom from*. But I now know that it is in fact better for me to exert my energy on *freedom for* i.e. knowledge.

**Man's development, the virtues:** It is very interesting to know that I am shaped by the choices I've made. And these choices are what define my virtues and vices. Not that I didn't have an idea of this before, but the classes I had on this really got me thinking. The only way I can be the man I want to be really starts with my choices. The consistency of this set of positive choices, then habits, turns into my virtues. Now I know where to invest my currency. With the way this course has influenced my life so far, it can only influence my future positively, whether in career or personal choices.

**Personal Choices:** This course will definitely affect my personal choices as regards the way I relate with people and who I decide to have a close relationship with. To start with, no human being is perfect, so my search for that perfect human being is ended.

Also, the things I go after in search for fulfillment will be intrinsic, yet finding a balance with extrinsic goods too. Because the truth is, extrinsic goods (which I have centered my efforts on) do not in themselves bring fulfillment.

**Career Choices:** My career choice is unchanged but modified. As an accountant, after knowing this much more about the nature of human beings, I will choose to make a conscious effort to understand the human aspect of everything we do.

## Yemisi Olomo

The "Nature of Human Beings" course has made me realize that I am the architect of my life and that ultimately the realization of my destiny is in my hands. I have learnt that I have the power to chart the course of my life and intend to consciously make wise choices. I have also learnt that there is room for development of good moral character but it can only be achieved with persistence.

In the area of studies, this course has made me develop an outlook that being a manager is not just about occupying a position, but also about recognizing the fact that I am a leader who is going to be responsible for others and will bring out the best in them if I treat them with respect and assist them to develop themselves.

In the area of career choice, this course has made me realize that a fat pay check should not be the sole reason for choosing a career.

## Ayoyemi Meigbope

The course in a short period has made me see things and, more importantly, human beings, differently. Before now, I used to react irrationally to issues because I just always assumed that everybody had to react to things in the same way I do and if I didn't get that result, it sometimes used to make me think negatively about the person or even take the person for granted. But now I see things differently and I have learnt to appreciate the different qualities that are unique to each individual. Also, it has made me have a rethink about my social attributes. I have learnt from the examples given and the experiences shared that no man can work alone without the support of other fellow individuals, since in most cases working as a team yields greater and more effective results.

I have been able to strike a great balance between my needs and my wants and I have realized through the course that most of the things I long for are the extrinsic goods that would not bring total fulfillment in the long run in the absence of the basic intrinsic goods. I have found out that the intrinsic goods are primary.

Considering the fact that as a human being I have the freedom to choose, I have come to realize that the choices I make to a great extent contribute to shaping my life. Also, it is clear that I am responsible for the rewards or the consequences of the choices I make in life.

I have also been able to work on and educate my emotions so that my intelligence will always play a larger role within me when I'm making decisions. Really! Also, I'm sure that, gradually, I will be able to work on some of the bad habits I currently have.

The knowledge I have acquired from this course will help me have better interpersonal relationships with people in every situation I find myself whether in my neighborhood, community, or office, etc.

Considering the fact that I want to be an entrepreneur, the knowledge gained from the course will help me relate well with my employees and know that each person in an organization or group is very different culturally and emotionally and has his/her own special contributions to make for the progress of an organization. I also hope to be able to impart the knowledge I have acquired from this course to other people.

## Bimbo Oke

The "Nature of Human Beings" course has really made me able to actually start to consciously think about how I treat fellow human beings. I now understand human beings better; I know that if I am to make someone do something there are ways to make the person do it with joy. This course has made me to see man as a rational being that has intelligence and will.

I now know that it is possible to act out of emotion and not necessarily think before acting. I am now working towards managing my emotions especially when I am angry. The fact that I acted in a particular way because I was angry does not make it right. I need to let my intelligence override my emotion and, although my emotions will still be there and should still take part in my actions, they should be handled with utmost care.

Furthermore, I learnt that if given freedom to choose or do as I please, I will be committed to my choices. I was able to trace back to some areas of my life where I had to be committed because I chose to follow that path and where I was not committed because I was forced and this caused a bit of delay in my academic career. This helped me to understand the power of choice and freedom in human beings; really I never thought of it until now.

I have also learnt to value friendship more, as you never know who might help you develop certain abilities. I am that kind of person that usually ends friendships at the point at which they start; I don't usually follow up on friends. I feel now that this is not right, as it portrays some degree of selfishness.

I also learnt about the intrinsic and extrinsic goods, I used to think of the monetary value of anything I wanted to do before actually doing it, to the extent that even when I really wanted to do something I would back off from it as long as it had no monetary value, but now I know better.

I have also learnt not to base my judgment about a person simply on what I feel as this is not always right. I do that a lot; I analyze people based on what I think about them.

In conclusion, I learnt some things about animals. I was surprised to know that we actually possess so many qualities in common with animals and if we do not put our own unique qualities into use while making decisions then we might just be making animalistic decisions.

This course will definitely help me in my personal and career choices in numerous ways. Starting with personal choices, this course will help me in my dealings with other human beings; it will definitely help me to understand every individual and not just judge the behavior of a person based on my personal feelings.

The course will influence my decisions since I know that human beings should not be manipulated. If you want someone to carry out a task it is better to make the person see reasons why he or she should do it rather than just commanding or giving tips (money) in order to make him or her happy as this will not bring out the best in him or her.

This course will also help me in my personal decision-making in the sense that since I now know that I cannot just change in my personal life by just wishing, I see the need to put in the necessary effort to educate my emotions and choose what to think and what to believe.

My personal decisions will also be influenced by this course in the sense that since I now know that the human beings are shaped by their choices, it is therefore important for me as an individual to be careful of the choices I make when carrying out my personal duties as these will definitely affect my values and what I believe in.

The principles of "freedom from" and "freedom for" will also affect my decisions as I now know that I should not let the fact that I am protecting my freedom from constraints affect my making an effort to achieve a "freedom for." I can see how a mistake in this aspect can actually destroy a person. My personal decisions will also be affected in the sense that I will be able to take responsibility for every decision I make even when it does not turn out the way I want. I now know that I have the power to choose. Even when it seems like there is no other option the truth is that in me there is actually a freedom of choice. It is therefore important for me as a person not to blame whatsoever wrong decision I make on anybody.

Careerwise this course will help me not to just focus on the actualization of material things or on monetary value when making decisions of where to work but to actually focus on self actualization as this is what will give me joy. It has also helped me to realize the fact of not having to restrict my choice to the concern of my personal interest alone but to also consider the interest of other people. Therefore when I start work in future or become a manager I will be able to understand the importance of making an impact in the lives of other people.

Considering that I want to be an entrepreneur later in life, this course has made me recognize that I have always to take into consideration the nature of human beings (people value their relations with others) and that I also have to maintain close interpersonal relationships with people. When I start work I must not see others merely as means to achieve my objectives as this can make people isolate themselves from me.

It is not possible for me to manipulate human beings when I start work or have my own business because I have realized that it is only a matter of time before that human being sees himself or herself as being manipulated and therefore strives for freedom. I will therefore always remember in future what I have learnt from this course and to always give people under me the opportunity to choose.

In the nearest future, careerwise, this course will definitely help me to remember to always make decisions based on my intelligence and not just on my feelings. The truth is that I will work to balance the two because naturally I am the kind of person that gets carried away by my feelings but I now know better. This will definitely help me to act better in any organization I find myself.

# CHAPTER 1

# Introduction

Human beings are very special beings, as we may have noticed at some point or the other in our lives. While speaking of organizations we generally refer to the people who work there as human resources. This terminology has not gone without criticism, very often justified, because of the tendency for firms to adopt an instrumental perspective of human beings as mere means for achieving the organization's goals. With that in mind, one could well understand and even expect a negative reaction to referring to people as human resources. Definitely people should not be seen as resources in the sense of assets acquired and owned and to be used. In the general meaning of the term, however, the word "resource" describes a person or thing that supplies help to another. It is in this sense that we can refer to people as resources, while being conscious of the limitations of the term. Thankfully, for a long time now, and each time more and more, management theory and practice reflects the appreciation that human resources are different from all other resources.

In workplaces, to achieve the organization's goals, one needs to work with other human resources, and, as a manager, one needs to work through other human resources. Unless we understand what human resources are and how we should treat them, we may face difficulties in achieving these goals. This book brings you a deeper knowledge and understanding of the nature of human beings, and particularly seeks to apply this knowledge to principles that make the person who embraces them a more responsible leader who can manage an organization ethically and sustainably for the common good of the society.

To start with, two brief real-life case studies illustrate the way human beings differ from the other resources of a firm, and then some basic concepts that will help in understanding and applying the contents of this book are explained. This is important because we do not always use words to mean the same concept, that is, the same word may call up different concepts depending on the way it is used. For example, the word "animal" is at times used in a way that excludes man, yet we all agree that biologically man is an animal. The word is being used analogically. This seems a good point to note that because we are attempting to understand human nature, and this is a reality above gender considerations, and it would be tedious to constantly say "he or she," "his or her," etc., and "he," "him," "his," and "himself" will be used here to represent both genders except when the context demands otherwise, such as when narrating or discussing specific case studies or both. Similarly, wherever the word "man" is used, depending on the context, both genders are implied.

There are four modules, and they are titled "Managing Oneself," "Working with Others," "Human Progress," and "The Full Picture." They contain 14 chapters, each of which tries to pass across some useful reflections on the nature of human beings and to draw some implications for responsible management with regard to ethics and sustainability. Many of the themes discussed may seem to be obvious. However, each reader will easily call to mind many current events worldwide that show us clearly that it is not as easy as it seems to understand and practice the consequences and yet that it is imperative that this be the case. Such is the challenge that faces every student of human nature. We feel that we know ourselves and others so well and yet each time we get surprises when we discover that we do not know so much after all.

Each chapter is structured in the same way: A brief introduction is followed by a real-life short case study and a coffee quiz, which comprises a few points to ponder on during the first "coffee break" that allows time for reflection and discussion. Concepts and principles of the nature of human beings are then explained and discussed. These discussions may be applied to the case study or to personal and professional experiences to draw out deeper knowledge of self and others. There are remarks offered (styled "coffee cues") to guide further dialogue and encourage further practical application of the case study, perhaps during a second "coffee break," and then there are exercises or projects followed by references suggested for further reading.

## Case 1: Exodus from Hepwhite

A tax analyst who used to work at Hepwhite Consulting was interviewing for a new job at Carmen & Associates. She was asked why she left her former employer, given her impressive qualifications, her broad experience, and the glowing signed recommendations she presented from several more senior colleagues.

She explained that during the financial crisis last year, several employees were laid off by the partners at Hepwhite, for reasons that most people considered flimsy. Everyone was aware that the firm had not lost any major client during the crisis and found it unfair to lay off employees that had worked hard. Even though the remaining employees were assured that their jobs were secure and were offered salary raises, most felt so upset about their friends that were involved in the lay-off that an air of unrest continued and the level of commitment to work dropped drastically. Suddenly, people started resigning. The firm recorded the highest rate of staff turnover ever during this period. When she saw that a good number of the people she worked with had gone, she decided to leave as well.

The interviewing committee stared at her incredulously. They could hardly believe their ears.

## Case 2: Annual Vacation

Fritz's boss was a very harsh, no-nonsense woman who prided herself in maintaining a business-like relationship at work. For her, one of the ways to do this was to never show emotion or concern when with her subordinates. She drove them tirelessly to perform excellently. However, despite all her diligent supervision, her unit always fell short of the management team's expectations regarding the monthly operational performance results. Their poor performance became a regular occurrence.

Last year, when she went on her annual vacation, another manager was deployed to the unit. This entirely different person showed some appreciation to every member of the team for his or her various contributions to the team. He listened to everyone's opinions and tried out some of their suggestions. During this period, they consistently exceeded the expectations of the management team.

The original manager came back and was very surprised that the same unit produced such an output. She convened a meeting where fortunately she asked the right questions and listened. She soon realized what had caused the leap in performance, and gradually she began to build a more humane relationship with her team. After an initial dip in the first month of her return, the performance indicators again swung upwards and continued improving over time.

## Coffee Quiz

1. You are the CEO at Hepwhite Consulting, and your friend, who is the senior partner at Carmen & Associates, has just told you the story of the tax analyst recently employed by his company after leaving yours. What are your thoughts on this?
2. What is the real difference between the two bosses Fritz's team had?

## Managerial Anthropology and Its Relevance

Anthropology is defined by *The New Oxford Dictionary of English* as "the study of humankind,"[1] especially of its origins, development, and customs and beliefs. While not intending to undertake a study so exhaustive, in order to study any aspect of the human race, we do need to know what the human being is. According to the same dictionary, humankind means "human beings considered collectively";[2] a human being is "a man, woman or child of the species *Homo sapiens*, distinguished from other animals by superior mental development, power of articulate speech and upright stance";[3] and a person is "a human being regarded as an individual."[4] Because managers are human beings, persons, and work with human beings, it is important for them to deeply understand themselves as such and also to understand the persons with whom they relate in order to be the best they can and to act in the manner that is most human. Within the pages of this book, we will attempt to enhance this understanding.

One of the classic definitions for a person is that of Boethius's: An individual substance of a rational nature.[5] The rational nature, which consists in the power to reason and to have ideas, sets man apart from other animals and from machines. It also bestows, on each person, a capacity for interiority, a capacity for dialogue (in order to communicate his ideas to others), a capacity to act according to a preferred idea, and a capacity to give of his or her individuality. Ideas being immaterial, they are evidence of an immaterialistic aspect of humans, and the inclinations to act according to ideas are also immaterial even though they can be influenced by one's physical or emotional state. These powers—of ideas (or thoughts) and of inclination (or willingness) based on ideas—make up the immaterialistic (or spiritual) aspect of a human being, which we at times refer to as the "mind," and make him able to discern and select from a variety of means and ends in order to achieve some purpose. He is able to know, reflect on his knowledge, understand, and choose from among the possibilities he has before him. Thus, it is from these powers that the notion of responsibility stems. We hold a man responsible for his actions because he understands and chooses what he does.

The choices we make have many consequences for ourselves and for those around us. Specifically, in the world of business, the choices of managers will affect themselves, the people who work with them, and the organization. Studying anthropology from a managerial perspective—that is, how to manage human beings including oneself—helps to empower managers who wish to be ethical and to run sustainable organizations to gain a knowledge that may help them to make optimal choices for achieving these goals.

The term "managerial anthropology" is scarce in management literature. One term very close to it would perhaps be "business anthropology." According to the *International Journal of Business Anthropology*, "business anthropologists play a key role in developing culturally sensitive policies and strategies in a world that increasingly typified by cross cultural contact."[6] Business anthropologists are also valuable to firms because they provide strategies for knowing customers better.[7] This is undoubtedly an important endeavour, as much for firms who simply wish to make profit as for those who are more oriented towards delivering value to their customers. In line with this, consultants in business anthropology study consumer behaviour and advise firms on their customers' characteristics and preferences.[8] As with many managerial techniques, this exercise can be used for noble or ignoble ends, as could happen in the case of a firm that studies its consumers' needs so as to provide for them or one that studies their weaknesses in order to manipulate them. Insights into this may provide interesting points of reflection for management students; however, this is not what is meant by the term "managerial anthropology" adopted in this book.

There is an aspect of business anthropology that concerns itself with human resources management and optimal workplace and work group practices.[9] In this sense, managers would be interested to know how human beings think, react, and function in order to get the best performance from their teams. Even if this interest is solely selfish, looking only to what is best for the firm, if the result is that employees are respected and given the consideration that is due to them as human beings with all their attendant rights, then the firm would have done something good. However, a firm that strives not to be merely good but really wishes to be the best it can be will also want to be a firm—a community of persons— where people who make up the firm at all levels strive to be the best they can be.[10] The only way that this can be achieved is by acting in the way that is most appropriate to what people really are, by projecting and bringing out the best of their human nature. What human nature really is then becomes is a good and indispensable guide for such a firm.

### Human Resource Management

The human resource function in an organization has a special responsibility towards the people who work in its organization. It is the responsibility of the human resource manager(s) to ensure that people are treated as befits them as people. A deep knowledge of human nature is essential for the human resource manager who wants to live up to this responsibility. At the same time, every manager in the firm who manages people is also participating to a large extent in human resource management and, therefore, needs the same science of who people are and the art of dealing with them appropriately, starting with his own self.

### Leadership

There has been much discussion about the differences between managers and leaders; some say that leaders need not be managers, and others say that not all managers are leaders.[11] What is clear is that those who have to manage people have to lead them in some way. In addition, a leader of an organization must be able to manage the people with whom he works, even if he does not relate directly with many people within the organization.

Hence, leader or manager, a deepened understanding of the human nature of people with whom one works means added leverage in knowing how to relate with them better and work better together. In particular, this knowledge makes a difference to one's ability to self-lead, as it constitutes an avenue to a richer self-knowledge.

The content of this text relates more to managing humans than any other resources, and this is why the term managers here can be used almost synonymously with leaders. They are not managers in this context because they manage a balance sheet, or the company's nonhuman assets, or the client accounts, etc., but rather with respect to the people they manage—more often than not, their subordinates, peers, and bosses. Thus, this book focuses on managers, but, from time to time, reference is made to leaders without in any way intending to separate them from the general category of those who have to lead and manage themselves and other people.

## Responsibility

Responsibility implies a call to answer for one's actions and their consequences, because they have been consciously or deliberately carried out. The etymology for "deliberate" is *de libero*, or out of free will. In the context of an organization, those who take decisions for the entity are responsible, albeit to different extents and in different ways, for those decisions, to different stakeholders—investors, creditors, customers, employees, unions (as spokesmen for employees), society, and the media (as spokesman for society). In order to be able to bear this responsibility, the person needs to constantly develop himself to be the best in order to give his best to those who are so reliant on him. A sense of responsibility is therefore a spur to take seriously the challenge of understanding oneself better in order to serve better.

## Sustainability

There are three aspects to sustainability—the social, environmental, and economic (the SEE) or what some like to call the people, planet, and profit approaches. Many people and businesses have gradually come to realize and admit—thanks especially to the work of many diligent scientists—that there have been many negative consequences to the planet from the activities of mankind and of businesses. These have come to constitute a threat to the future of the planet. At the same time, the world is more and more aware of social inequalities—First and Third Worlds, etc.—and of the need to distribute more equitably the wealth that is being created. At the root of all this are visible cracks in the economic models on which the world has run unquestioningly for decades, and scholars and practitioners are now working to repair those cracks, to rebuild the framework, and to create new models. Understanding ourselves better and therefore knowing how to manage ourselves optimally is a good foundation to be able to manage others around us better and also to manage the earth's resources in a way that preserves them for the present and future generations of human beings who share our nature.

## Human Nature

The previous considerations are an indication of the rising importance of understanding human nature better, in order to know how to lead oneself and others, to know what a human being can be responsible for, and to know in which direction one can develop oneself and others sustainably. Human nature, according to the dictionary, comprises the "general characteristics, feelings, and behavioral traits of humankind, regarded as shared by humans."[12] This is a fairly good description of the subject matter of this book, which is aimed at deepening our comprehension of human nature.

Knowing what something is helps us to know how best to treat it and how best to preserve it. When that something is valuable, it is even more imperative to study it and ensure that it is taken care of in a way that respects and conserves its nature. A humor video clip that may be familiar to some of us is that in which a woman happily watches her little girl doing the washing up, and then her proud smile turns into a horrified scream as she realizes that it is her laptop that the child is so carefully washing in the kitchen sink. The child continues singing a ditty, blissfully ignorant of what has happened to her mother's precious possession.

This applies to the way we treat ourselves as human beings, to the way we treat other human beings whom we come across or impact during our lifetimes, and to the way we treat the world we live in as our habitat. If we can respect the laws of nature on these three levels, we will be able to evaluate our actions with a view to striving constantly to behave in a good way and in the right way, to behave ethically.

### Ethical Behavior

Ethical behavior is appropriate to human nature because it demonstrates intelligent action. We only talk of ethical behavior when speaking of human beings. This is because we intuitively know that human beings are the only earthly beings that can reason, and therefore, choose their actions according to their end in view. We have the possibility of reflecting at what has been called a second-order level[13] on our own ideas and wishes in order to carry them out deliberately. Animals do not reach this second-order level. Thus, we do not consider the ethics of the behavior of bees or stones. These beings always act according to the law of their nature by default. We do not blame them for their actions. What they do is always good[14]—they cannot do otherwise. It would be absurd to try, convict, and imprison a monkey for throwing stones and breaking windscreens for the enjoyment it derives from it.

Humans on the other hand are able to decide how to act, so if they cause harm or damage they are held responsible for it. Perhaps this is why we speak of an action being "premeditated" when discussing its gravity; in contrast to this, animals do not plan or premeditate. We are able to make a judgment of the intellect, a second-order reflection, known as conscience, which compares our past, present, and future actions with our own idea of what is good or bad. If we have a wrong idea of what is good or bad, we will unfortunately make a wrong judgment. Hence, the importance of learning what is really good and not just what is good for me or what is good for me now.

A broader outlook and a more long-term outlook could help here. Even if I think that what is good for me now is to spend extra hours in bed, realizing that I will miss the school bus, arrive late, have to catch up on my own with missed schoolwork, and so on, may help me to readjust my idea of what is good. Sadly, if I neglect what my conscience tells me is good, my intellect is likely to end up attempting to justify my inclination (as our intellect and will are not separate entities but fully united) and the process tends to dull the conscience. I will find it easier to stay in bed tomorrow if I stay in bed today because I will have found good reasons for justifying staying in bed, and my conscience will protest less. When this is applied to an organization, which could have much higher potential to harm people—employees, consumers, shareholders, society, the environment—the ramifications are easily imaginable.

This is also why we can speak of what we do as ethical or unethical with respect to how much it fits into what is good for man whether with reference to the individual, to the society, or to the race. What is good for the human race could be considered by looking at the effects of our actions on present generations and based on this, making equitable decisions, or by looking at their effects on future generations, and therefore, making sustainable decisions. In both cases, our choices are more ethical, and we display more awareness that we are responsible for them.

## Coffee Cues

The two cases are indicative of the benefits of communicating the worth of one's subordinates to them. One can only do this if in the first place one understands the worth of a human being. In the first case, we see a situation in which people value the way their colleagues are treated above financial rewards, while, in the second, the same set of people achieve a different level of performance because of the way they are treated. It is important not to undermine people's worth; it is important that managers create a conducive working environment where their subordinates can share their opinions and in this way demonstrate their talents and potentials. Understanding human nature helps one to create the appropriate environment for human beings to thrive and to excel.

## Project

Think of a recent ethical scandal, global or local, in the business world—LIBOR, GlaxoSmithKline, Siemens, British Petroleum—and begin to analyze it in terms of each chapter of this book. Meet with coursemates or your lecturer in small groups to discuss your insights into what really happened in the case you chose, and record what new ideas you get from them.

Follow the thread of the news (past, present, and future) in the different media on this event and people's reaction to it.

By the end of the course you should have a full anthropological reflection on this event. Present your analysis to the class. Together with your lecturer, select and prepare a segment for publication.

# MODULE 1

# Managing Oneself

# CHAPTER 2

# The Human Manager

The human being is a life form that inhabits the earth. The human being is you and I. Around us there are many other life forms and we share some characteristics with all of them. Just the fact of being on earth is common to everything that is here. In order to fully understand ourselves, we need to also understand the world in which we live.

Among the things that exist, those that have life have some good that the others do not have. This is because they possess something that the lifeless beings do not have, that is, life, and so we could say that animals have a perfection that inanimate beings do not have. If we refer to different possible attributes as perfections—life, growth, movement, etc.—it is in this sense that we could compare two beings with regard to the perfections they possess. Thus, for example, a cat has more perfections than a stone. Whereas the cat possesses the perfections of the stone—matter occupying space and time, the cat has other perfections that the stone does not have—life manifested in certain operations: growth, movement, excretion, respiration, reproduction, nutrition, irritability, or sensitivity, etc. Among life forms, there is also a hierarchy more or less based on the existence and level of complicatedness of the said operations. Broadly speaking therefore, among life forms, we have a division into two categories—plants and animals, where plants lack some of the operations that animals have.

Human beings have many perfections in common with other animals and also have a few critical perfections that set them apart from the other animals and all other living beings on the earth. This is why one of the earliest definitions,[1] that of Aristotle, of what is a human being is specifically based on the point of difference—that man is a rational animal.[2] All animals have sense knowledge but man has intellective knowledge as an additional level of knowledge to the sensitive[3] level—he has the power of understanding with the use of non-sensible[4] concepts, that is, ideas. He can engage in abstraction, reflection, judgment, analysis, and all those activities that in general we term "thinking." Since an activity ought to have a pro-portionate cause, man's thinking activity, which is above the bodily or material order, must be done by something that is nonbody or spiritual. Thus, the realization that man engages in intellectual thought leads us to conclude that he has a spiritual soul that possesses the nonmaterial faculty by which he thinks and reasons and is therefore able to choose what is the best for him. We call his ability to choose freedom, and in it lies his dignity.

Having a rational nature means that man knows and wills in a way that the other animals cannot. As explained in the introduction, this aspect of man is immaterial (spiritual).[5] Yet, man remains an animal and we cannot forget this if we want to understand ourselves and others. When we use the expression "he is only human," we often refer precisely to this fact that man is an animal, that is, made of flesh and blood and having the emo-tions and passions that can overcome his rational faculties. The human manager is only human after all. In this chapter, we discuss the character-istics we share with other living beings, in particular with other animals.

## Case: You Should be Above That!

The Christmas and New Year holidays were over, and Kweku was back from his leave. He had been granted a 2-week leave of absence. One after-noon when I was at home, I heard the sound of a car horn. This person blew the horn a number of times but there was no response from within. As always, I thought Kweku should be there to open the gate. The car horn sounded again, until I had heard it about five times. So, I stepped out of the house to know who was at the gate. First, I called Kweku's name to know if he was around and on getting no response I proceeded to the gate. I looked through the little opening in the gate to discover it was my father who was there. He was back quite early and I wondered why but, more importantly, I wondered why Kweku was not available to open the gate. I opened the gate and he drove in. He looked angry, and he expressed it, given the amount of time he had spent outside. Though it was the duty of the gatekeeper to open the gate, he was very angry with me and at the absence of the gatekeeper. Surely he must have had a rough day, I thought.

The following day, the same thing happened again. Kweku was not at his duty post. My father drove in after I had opened the gate, angry again.

This time though, he expressed his anger at the absence of Kweku only. That evening, he sent me to call Kweku into the house. He wanted to talk to him. Kweku came in, but he did not get the opportunity to speak. My dad just vented his anger at him all through the meeting. He concluded with a warning note to sack him if the "ugly incidents" continued.

The day after, Kweku still was not at his duty post when my father came back. This time around I thought that his job was over. This is because my father rarely gets upset but when he gets into a rage as he did the day before, he means everything he says. That evening, to my amazement when he sent for Kweku, he did not sack him. He simply asked him why he had not been at his duty post during those times he had arrived home. The younger man then proceeded to narrate his story:

> His aged father was ill, and he had already spent a huge part of his income trying to treat him. The man was getting better but there were some medications and hospital bills that were yet unpaid. He (Kweku) would have come directly to my father to request that he be paid in advance, but he had already received 4 months' pay in advance, which my father would be deducting in fractions from his monthly package. Thus, he could not approach my father for any more advances. He explained that he had been leaving the compound during a certain part of the day to a neighbor's house to help with cleaning the compound, and washing the cars. He had to do this to earn a little extra to send home for his father's bills.

At the end of the story, my father simply heaved a sigh. He empathized with Kweku. Surprisingly, he also apologized for his uncivil behavior the day before, for not giving Kweku the opportunity to speak. This time around, he did not give him money as an advance payment but asked for the exact amount that was left unpaid. Kweku responded. At this, my father asked me to fetch his checkbook from his office bag. He wrote a check to cover the amount, adding a little extra for Kweku.

Since that incident, we have never had such an incident of Kweku leaving his duty post without prior permission from either me or my father. Even better, the relations between him and my dad have improved.

## Coffee Quiz

1. What happened to the narrator's father after the first two incidents? What happened to Kweku?
2. What do you think about the title of the case; who should be above what?

## Sense Knowledge and Experience

Like all other animals, we humans get to know things through our five external senses—the senses of taste, touch, hearing, smell, and sight. Whatever we know today must have first been perceived through those senses before being processed into what we have stored in our minds. These five senses take information from the external world to feed to the person and to build up experiences that determine what is afterwards inside the person. At the most basic level, one could think of how whatever is pleasant in the external environment filters through the senses to the innermost part of the person and affects his level of comfort. For example, a clean, nice-smelling environment that is well decorated could probably contribute to help people be more cheerful and work better. Aesthetics do matter. Noise levels affect comfort, for example, in factories, etc. A hard and uncomfortable chair can affect work output.

Responses to stimuli, such as snatching one's hand away from a source of intense heat or looking up when one hears a noise, etc., are also a reality of human life. They reach us through our senses and our sensitivity (or irritability) kicks in. With time to think, one can overcome or moderate response to a given stimulus, for example, by determinedly applying a hot compress to a sprain or steeling oneself to ignore noise and interruption. However, it is probably advantageous to an organization to bear this in mind and seek to minimize the possibility of distractions at work for their employees and to provide favorable stimuli that could challenge them to innovate and improve at work.

Our senses can be impaired. They can also be mistaken. How many times has one believed that one saw something or someone, only to be corrected and to realize that it was a mistake? Impairment or mistakes in the sense perception do not make anyone a lesser human being or unworthy of being treated with as much dignity as any other. They should only make us more aware of our limitations and therefore more careful in looking at things from all possible sides and calmly. They should also make us more understanding of others' limitations.

There are many implications of considerations regarding the dignity of man, discussed in the introductory chapter, and our possibilities of error due to physical limitations, mentioned earlier. Only two will be mentioned here. The first is that we owe respect and consideration to everyone regardless of whatever impairment they may have. The second is that we should be able to accept our own or others' mistakes and failures, learn from them, and move on. The first is important in developing openness to diversity and readiness for inclusion, critical for managing people, and the second in achieving the resilience that is needed to survive in a harsh business environment.

## Basic Instincts and Intuition

When I was growing up in Ibadan,[6] in my parents' house we reared many different animals at different times. I remember a flock of guinea fowls. They would walk around the compound in single file, whether on the ground or on the surrounding fence. When the guinea fowls laid their eggs, if we wanted them to hatch, my parents would take the eggs from the guinea fowl's nest (invariably she would not be there) and put them in the nest of a brooding hen, taking away the hen's own eggs. The hen would sit on the eggs until they hatched, and then mother the baby guinea fowls until they were old enough to fend for themselves. It made an incongruous picture each time—a hen leading her brood of guinea fowls around the compound!

The reason for doing things that way was that the guinea fowl's mothering instinct is generally quite feeble, and so it would not sit on the eggs till they hatched. The chances of an egg's survival to hatching were therefore low if it was left to itself. Hens, on the other hand, will never abandon their eggs till they hatch; witness the hen's patience to sit on the guinea fowl's eggs no matter how long it took. In fact, chickens hatch in a considerably shorter time than guinea fowls; this is why the hen's own eggs had to be removed. If anything hatched, the hen's brooding instinct would expire and she would stand up and leave the nest. The hen would never notice whether they were her eggs or not, or whether they were her chicks or not; she would simply act on her instincts and hatch them and lead them round as she would have in any case. It was in this way that we were able to keep breeding guinea fowls.

All animals have some inbuilt instincts. This is why one may react instinctively in some situations—the instinct to run from perceived danger when one hears a scream, without waiting to know what is happening, or a mother's instinct to put on the baby's oxygen mask before hers,[7] or a baby's instinct to suck breast milk. Instincts are generally there for the preservation of the species—rules within nature that help to avoid danger and to do what is needed to survive.

All animals have sense memory. This is instinct informed by experience. For example, sheep will flee from a wolf. Rats will avoid the place where another rat was caught by a trap. Some human instincts are less powerful than the equivalent in animals because we also have intellectual memory. Thus, for example, a man may instinctively feel like fleeing from a wolf, but will be able to pause, even if momentarily, and reflect on whether he has some means to get rid of the wolf—scare it away, disable or even kill it, whether he could get help, etc.

In addition to sense memory, man has intuition. The dictionary defines intuition as "the ability to understand something immediately, without the need for conscious reasoning";[8] one feels strongly that something is true without knowing why. Experiences in the past subconsciously could make us tend to anticipate the significance of future events without knowing how. Thus, one might intuitively feel that this is the right choice to make to arrive at one's goal. A mother could intuitively sense that her child is in danger, without knowing why this conviction has come to her. As our senses and past experiences could be mistaken, intuition is also not infallible. Very often however, it is a good guide for some kinds of action, even in making managerial decisions. For other kinds of action, it may not be enough to rely on intuition.

## Memory and Imagination

These are two internal senses that we share with other animals, though they are on a different level in man. They are not fully under our control.

For example, we sometimes remember what we would prefer to forget and forget what we would prefer to remember. There are practices that help one to gain more control over memory. These are useful only to the extent that they result in good effects for the human being—this will further be discussed in Chapter 6.

In a similar way, the imagination could at times be unruly. When it is tamed and harnessed, it serves in one's work, for example, to enhance creativity and innovation or to understand others. However, when it is left to run wild, it can give rise to many problems, for example, fears conjured up could cause timidity and make a person overly risk-averse. This could at the very least hamper productivity when a person is expected to use initiative and display ownership in his work— whether self-employed or working in a firm owned by others.

## Commonness and Uniqueness of Human Nature

One very important conclusion from the earlier reflections in this chapter is that each human being is in the end the same, since we have a common nature with regard to what defines us as human and separates us from animals. Thus, due to the fact that we all have the same dignity of persons, individuals of humankind, all humans are equal. In the next three chapters, we will reflect on more similarities at the level of the emotions and passions and then go into what differentiates humans from other animals. These next three chapters lay the foundation for appreciating the uniqueness of each human being while still discussing what is common to every human being.

In this chapter, so far, we have deliberately not gone into the details of all the many and varied physical, psychological, and mental operations that are written into the nature of human beings as is paralleled with other animals, because it is impossible to do this exhaustively, but it is good to be aware of them. Thus, for example, our processes for breathing and excretion go on despite us, our dependence on food or our subjection to gravity must be overcome with special effort if we care to go against it, our body suffers pain when deprived of its natural protection, etc.

The awareness of the human body and its needs and realities demands from a firm the sensitivity to put in place whatever safety and health policies and procedures are necessary; to ensure that there is adequate air and water supply for all employees, especially factory workers, and to ensure stress levels are kept under control. A living being needs a suitable ecosystem if it is to thrive: comfortable or orthopedic chairs, especially for those who sit for long because of the demands of their jobs, screen protection for those who use computers heavily, etc. Leave periods are needed for people to recover their strengths both intellectually and bodily. As a popular pidgin English saying puts it, *"body no be wood."*[9] Organizations that treat their staff as if they were tables and chairs and have no need to rest or to have adequate surroundings to flourish in will not be doing right and may face negative consequences resulting from their neglect. After all, Maslow's hierarchy of needs model[10] is a recognition of the dual composition of man—his animal and his rational sides—and one level has to be attended to in order to adequately prepare the person for operating optimally in the next. Each person needs to understand these facts about himself in order to avoid pushing himself too hard and then suffering the consequences of a physical, psychological, or mental collapse.

In fact, there are cost savings also to the firm for doing these things—from reduced health costs and absenteeism, etc. There are also benefits from having greater job and organizational satisfaction leading to a happier and more committed workforce.

## Coffee Cues

In the first conversation in the aforementioned case study, the narrator's father appears to have at first suspended the possibility of a rational conversation and simply vented his anger as it came. Kweku reacted by not appealing to reason either. The narrator and his father had forgotten to look at Kweku as an individual and gotten used to merely seeing him as one more resource working mechanically. The incident finally made them remember that he was a human being like themselves and now they could imagine what had happened to him and feel for him.

# Exercises

Try to think of three actions you performed recently that were greatly determined by sense experience, by instinct or intuition, or by memory and imagination. Now can you think of any action that was not influenced even remotely by any of these and was purely rational?

Try to forget something that keeps coming to your mind. For example, can you forget (at least for a week) the sting of that wounding remark from the girl you asked out to dinner last week and the five possible apt rejoinders you should have given and did not manage to come up with because you were too upset to think?

# CHAPTER 3

# The Beginning of Self-Management

The feeling part of human nature, which this chapter deals with, is very complex. According to Reichmann (1985), "an emotional experience is a complex internal activity involving an intense and spontaneous appetitive and somatic response to a psychic awareness."[1] Humans share the emotional aspect of their nature with animals. Despite this, most emotions are developed to a higher degree in human beings; thus, the way we say that a dog feels sad is probably not the same as the way we say that a girl feels sad; and we hardly would ever say that a chicken feels sad. This is not because one has anything against a dog or a chicken, but merely because one realizes and accepts a difference in the level of perfection (the meaning of this word was explained in the introduction) and therefore of the capacity for sadness of each of these three animals.

Emotions are experienced with different intensities and durations. Due to these differences, we at times label them differently—referring in different contexts to feelings, passions, a temperament, moods, appetites, etc. A more general classification could be based on those differences in intensity and duration such that a very intense but transitory emotion would be called a passion; a less intense but longer lasting emotion would be termed a feeling; an emotion whose duration is neither long nor short and is of moderate intensity would be called a mood; a relatively stable emotional tendency would be called a temperament; and a short burst of emotion in response to a perceived good would be called an appetite. All of them are often expressed with the verb "to feel" in common language. Understanding how they each and all play out in oneself is the beginning of self-management.

Within this text, we could propose the following examples for varying types of emotions.

Feelings (at times used synonymously with emotions in all their forms): Sadness, Envy, Resentment, Hope, Fear, Despair, Malice, Compassion, Benevolence, Sympathy.

Passions: Love, Hatred, Anger, Vengefulness, Jealousy, Greed, Grief

Appetites: Hunger, Thirst, Lust.

Moods: Irritability, Cheerfulness, Happiness, Despondence, Solitude, Optimism, Pessimism.

Temperaments: Melancholy, Sanguineness, Choler, Phlegm.

Merely looking at the variety of description and examples above already gives the sense that we have before us here a complicated reality. Each human being has to deal with all these within his own self and try to harness them all to work toward his individual good while respecting the good of those around him. When organizations full of people who are each trying to manage themselves then set out to manage these people, it is not surprising that it is not an easy task. Emotions are separate from the mind, that is, emotions do not reason, and so people could at times seem unreasonable because they are being emotional. Yet, beneath what appears to be irrational behavior, there is often an underlying logical sequence that a careful manager could have expected and detected by taking the existence and the influence of emotions into account.

## Case: Exodus from Hepwhite

A tax analyst who used to work at Hepwhite Consulting was interviewing for a new job at Carmen and Associates. She was asked why she left her former employer, given her impressive qualifications, her broad experience, and the glowing signed recommendations she presented from several more senior colleagues.

She explained that during the financial crisis last year, several employees were laid off by the partners at Hepwhite, for reasons which most people considered flimsy. Everyone was aware that the firm had not lost any major client during the crisis and found it unfair to lay off employees who had worked hard. Even though the remaining employees were assured that their jobs were secure and were offered salary raises, most felt so upset about their friends who were involved in the layoff that an air of unrest continued and the level of commitment to work dropped drastically. Suddenly, people started resigning. The firm recorded the highest rate of staff turnover ever during this period. When she saw that a good number of the people she worked with had gone, she decided to leave as well.

The interviewing committee stared at her incredulously. They could hardly believe their ears.

## Coffee Quiz

1. Why were the interviewers surprised?
2. Did Hepwhite Consulting "shoot itself in the foot"? What could the management have done to handle the situation better?
3. What should Carmen and Associates learn from this incident?

## Appetition, Feelings, and Emotions

As already suggested above, appetition is a temporary movement of the passions or emotions. It is usually directed toward some perceived good. This good could be material or immaterial (spiritual). What we strictly call emotions are more permanent than feelings, yet they are also temporary. Moods are graduations of emotions. People who feel things keenly are said to be more emotional. People who are more emotional could tend to be moody or "temperamental" if they do not attempt to control or educate their emotions. This is discussed further below.

Emotions aid our survival and help us to live a rich life. They serve to communicate to others what we have within—a smile to encourage or convey approval, a frown to show displeasure, etc. They can help to stimulate interest in a task that would otherwise be boring. When we feel good, we work well and we communicate the sense of wellbeing to the people around us so that they also feel good. When we find an undertaking difficult or daunting, stimulating emotions can help to build up the drive to take on the challenge or to keep at it. They buoy us up to face danger; for example, soldiers going to battle need to feel anger at the enemy. It could be easier to help friends than to help mere acquaintances.

## Passions and Temperament

Nature, character, personality, disposition, temper, spirit, outlook, makeup, and humor are sometimes used interchangeably as if they meant the same thing. In fact, they do not. Since they cannot be totally isolated and scrutinized—a person acts with a mixture of all of them in play—as if each existed on its own, it is usual to speak loosely of one when referring to one or more of the others. There are excellent essays and works that have distinguished and explained these realities[2] and, out of interest, one could consult these and read further about them. For our purpose, it is enough to realize that human beings legitimately have different temperaments and as such should be respected and accommodated as they are. Yet, it is critical to realize that since they operate below the wavelength of reason, we have to work on these emotions in order that they do not lead us to make suboptimal choices that are not the best for the total human being. The emotions in themselves only react based on what reaches the senses; the whole human being is more than just a bundle of senses. His dignity lies precisely in having a nature that is above the merely material, and therefore when he acts on the merely material or animal level, he will be acting below his dignity and ultimately will be harming himself and others who receive the impact of his actions.

## Education, Self-mastery, and Sensitivity

Educating the emotions increases objectivity in and control of one's reactions. From this perspective, having a good handle on one's emotions is a great strength. The good handle is developed by practicing mastery of the emotions in small things that do not seem to matter much. This is the way to develop a habitual control of the emotions and to educate them not to overrun the person. Thus, for example, a person who struggles to moderate a craving for chocolate or to delay taking her lunch for 3 minutes even if she is very hungry, will find it easier to control her temper when an infuriating email arrives from a colleague. Her emotions would have "learnt" that they cannot always have their own way, and she would be displaying self-mastery.

When the emotions are in their place, they operate as a help to achieve the person's goal. The person manifests them at the right time. For example, a manager would need to display sympathy when a colleague receives bad news at work. Even if the manager is very happy at some personal achievement, concern for others and self-mastery would make it possible to empathize with the other person and share the other person's feelings and show the solidarity that he needs at that moment. Another example could be in the event that one wishes to encourage one's team in difficult circumstances when one is in fact feeling discouraged oneself. In spite of the difficulties in the economic environment, a good team leader can inspire his people by displaying optimism and courage and showing them these by word and by example.

Beyond managing one's own emotions, one also needs to be sensitive to the emotions of other people. This is the skill sometimes referred to as emotional intelligence and it is very important in relating to others. The ability to read others' emotions and respond to them accordingly makes a person a very valuable member of a team, organization, or society. Such a person will be able to build rich and lasting relationships with others and therefore able to work better with them to achieve joint goals. Conversely, an insensitive person would tend to walk over people because he would not perceive their feelings, and therefore, consciously or unconsciously, he would alienate those who could have worked together with him and eventually this would harm the organization. Often, where there is such a manager, the organization could find itself faced with sudden problems that a more sensitive manager would have noticed and nipped in the bud, for example, a strike action, a mass uproar, a breakdown in client negotiations, a conflict with regulators or other government authorities, a media disaster, etc.

## Interior Freedom

When the person is ruled by emotions, it is difficult to have an experience of true freedom. Freedom belongs to a realm above the emotions and therefore emotions need to be guided and elevated by a powerful intellect and will for a person to be truly free and responsible. As man is a being that develops habits, if one repeatedly allows the emotions to take over, it becomes more and more the default reaction and less and less easy to allow reason to have an upper hand. This is why it is important to understand one's emotions and avoid becoming enslaved by them by allowing them to override what the intellect and the will point out as the way to exercise freedom.

A manager who habitually loses his temper and does not try to control it, saying perhaps *"I'm hot-tempered; that's how I've always been; they should learn,"* will find his temper taking over even when he does not want it to. He might lose it for instance in a board meeting, or in a meeting to negotiate with critical suppliers. Such a person becomes less free; he has constrained his power of choosing how he wants to behave by ceding his self-control to his passions. The organization will find it more difficult to rely on such a person.

In a similar way, a person who allows resentments, jealousies, envies, moods, etc. to affect interaction with colleagues or efficient application to the task at hand will be doing the organization a disservice. The more the person gives in to these sentiments, the more difficult it will be for the person to resist the temptation to allow them free rein and therefore the less free the person will be to judge issues and carry out actions reflectively and objectively. His interior freedom would have been lost or at the very least compromised. With discipline, he could gradually become freer from being carried away by his emotions and enhance his ability to embrace the future free from the encumbrance of useless baggage.

## Communication

In sending messages across to others, we need to realize that emotions are also vehicles of messages. People around us communicate their emotional state, readiness to work, apprehensions, fears, excitement, etc. and taking these into account could make work easier. A boss who does not notice the emotions of his subordinates will lose a lot of information that could have helped the team to work together better.

Inadvertently, we can communicate wrong or mixed messages. Imagine that one is saying yes with a surly expression—something is showing that is contrary to what is being said. This is why, at times, once we are reassured that the emotion displayed did not tally with what the person really meant, we should allow it to pass and ensure it does not affect future interactions with that person. For example, a person might respond in anger to a question and later explain that he was not angry but had just received upsetting news at that moment. One can understand and not let any bad feeling linger, once one understands that this is quite possible.

## Coffee Cues

The partners at Hepwhite may have had in mind the model of the economically rational man who seeks to maximize his self-interest all the time, and so they expected the remaining employees to protect their own jobs by putting in more effort and to be happy they would have higher salaries, particularly in a period of economic turbulence. They were proved wrong. Probably to their surprise, people set aside financial stability and, despite the scarcity of jobs due to the economic recession, chose to resign rather than stay in a firm that could act so callously. They felt bad for their colleagues and acted on those emotions, proving that human beings are not always economically rational and that economic rewards are not always enough to motivate employees. "Maximizing profit," "optimizing utility," or "attaining career progression" is not a term that can explain a human being fully. This also applies in spheres of life other than in the workplace, for example, one could choose to shop at a more expensive location due to personal relationships developed over time or simply a superior aesthetic experience.

## Exercises and Project

Call to mind a recent experience at work. Separate the emotional from the other components.

Draw up a "Sad-Glad-Mad" table (see example below) of all the emotions you can call to mind and write down how they are expressed. The table could start as follows:

| Emotion | Expression | Emotion | Expression | Emotion | Expression |
|---------|-----------|---------|-----------|---------|-----------|
| Sad | Tears | Glad | Smiles | Mad | Frown |

*(Continued)*

*(Continued)*

Below sad, write down words that describe feelings that approximate "sad," such as "weepy," "desolate," and "sorry." In the next column, write beside each one some indications that you might notice in a colleague or classmate that could express that feeling, such as "tears," "distraction," or "an apology note." Do the same for "glad" and "mad."

During the next 3 weeks, struggle not to speak when upset or angry, even internally to yourself. At the end of the period, try to calculate the percentage of times you succeeded out of all the incidents, for each of the 3 weeks.

Think back to the last time when someone annoyed you and try to step out of yourself and think why. Check if you could have been in any way the cause of the other person's negative reaction to you.

# CHAPTER 4

# Abstraction and Reflection

This chapter is about the knowing part of human nature and its implications for responsible leadership, ethics, and sustainability. Human beings are above other animals in two ways. One of them is our ability to know intellectually and the other is our ability to choose, to will. Both of them constitute human rationality and make us free. As already discussed earlier, there are acts that we do not have control over, such as our digestion, giving in to the force of gravity, etc., but we could consider that these are not, strictly speaking, human acts, since they only involve our animal capabilities rather than our whole selves. Our whole selves include our thinking and willing faculties.

A man is able to know. Using the term loosely, we can of course also say that animals know; in the way that we say that a dog knows its master and a chicken knows when the time for roosting has come. Animals, including man, have senses and therefore they have the knowledge that comes through the senses and to different extents, depending on the perfection of their brains, they can process this sense knowledge in some way. However, man knows both at this level and at a higher level. We know things and we abstract from what we know through reflecting on what has come to us through the senses. For this we use a power that only man has—the intellect. Hence, if in the concept of knowledge we include abstraction and reflection, then among all animals, only man knows. He goes beyond instincts and sense knowledge to intellectual knowledge.

Here is an example of how we know. We learn from when very young what a chair is. As we grow up, we meet different kinds of chairs and each time this strengthens the concept of "chair" that is already formed in the mind. Very soon we can think of "chair" without having any chair around us. We can construct a chair in our minds. We can use the concept in many ways just with our immaterial thoughts. We have grasped the essence of what makes a chair a chair and not anything else, what you could call the "chairness" of the chair. More than this, we are even able to grasp intangible realities[1] and unreal concepts[2]. The limitless power of abstraction and reflection is accompanied by a capacity to make judgments connecting different concepts and different judgments and thus to reason.

This is very interesting for managing people: each human being has this power just by being human, and therefore each one has an unlimited capacity for intellectual knowledge. Knowing this helps us to understand the relevance of training, of discussing with people what their job entails and not simply expecting them to work like machines, of not taking people for granted, of understanding that people continue thinking long after a transaction is completed, of appreciating intellectual work, of understanding the need, when involved in job design, that people have for their work to have a component that appeals to their intellect, etc. It also underlines the need to explain things to people, to engage their minds and not only their hands, to reason with subordinates when you wish them to buy into new ideas or the company's values, of preparing all types of communication well in a way that is logical and respectful of the people who will receive these messages, etc. New policies such as ethical codes, sustainability mandates, etc. need to be explained well to those who are to implement them, confident in their ability to read beyond the letter to the spirit of the instructions given by the management team. Ignoring this human attribute can have consequences—condescension, micromanaging, disrespect, etc.—as we shall see in the case of Mansoor.

## Case: Mansoor

Mansoor, a resourceful and experienced advertising professional, who had worked on the agency side his entire career, suddenly became consumed with a burning desire to experience life on the client side of the business. This happens occasionally to young professionals in a service industry—they develop a craving to cross over to a client role. The clients are usually in the banking, telecoms, oil and gas, or fast-moving consumer goods industries. The enticement to cross over includes a better remuneration and status perks, and a longing to possess the perceived power exercised by clients in dictating the job and its pace to the service company.

In due course, Mansoor was able to realize his ambition; he got a brand management role in a multinational manufacturing firm.

He threw himself into the job with much excitement, full of fervor and zeal, eager to make his mark quickly and impress his employers and his coworkers. However, this initial fervor did not last long. He soon realized that his "creativity" was not reckoned with in his new role. More emphasis was placed on thinking in a rigid sequence and discipline in following laid-down procedure. In advertising agencies, employees had been required to be creative and to engage in lateral thinking!

Mansoor complained to his new colleagues that he was feeling stifled. His boss got to know of this and was displeased. He told Mansoor in no uncertain terms that what was required of him was to simply follow laid-down procedure, that the operational strategy for all outposts/operations across the globe emanated from the global headquarters overseas and that if he continued to sow discontent among staff he would be dismissed. Mansoor was very disappointed. He was earning much more money than ever before and occupied a prestigious position, yet he was frustrated by the realization that he was to become a figurehead of sorts and had to rein in his thinking capabilities.

In addition, he sorely missed the warmer and informal interpersonal relationships he had with his colleagues in the advertising agency, as opposed to the "arms-length" relationships he observed within the multinational corporation. After a while, he no longer looked forward to going to the office each morning.

After 16 "harrowing" months, to the shock of his bosses and of a number of friends and acquaintances, he resigned from the multinational company and reapplied for his old job. His previous employers were only too happy to regain the expertise of a tested and trusted hand.

He had to settle for a pay slash, but he was very happy to be back in an environment in which one's ideas were welcome, tested, refined, and applied, and where friendships thrived. He felt he was again making contributions that impacted both the company and its clients positively. Thus, he was happy.

## Coffee Quiz

1. What happened to Mansoor?
2. What kind of job design might have made him stay on in the manufacturing company?
3. What considerations could possibly make you accept a lower paying job or at a less prestigious company?

## Intellect and Intellectual Experience

As we have seen in Chapter 1, man is a rational animal. Every human being has an intellect. The intellect works through the brain. Since the brain is a material organ, it could happen that it is impaired. If this were to happen, the person's intellect might not be able to function at its full potential. However, this would not make this person less of a human being or less worthy in any way of full respect for his human dignity. The difference between this person and others would be the extent and the nature of his intellectual experience, not the fact of having an intellect. Just as no human being has every experience possible to the species and continues nevertheless being a fully human person, the same applies in this case. To make it even clearer, people differ in capacity for aesthetic experience; for sense experience, for example, a blind man; and for mental, athletic, physical, or sensual experience without this suggesting any inequality in dignity as humans.

This could be illustrated with the idea of an overhead tank meant to supply water through a tap. If the tap malfunctions and the water fails to get through, it does not mean that the water is not there. It is simply unable to pass through because of a secondary reason. This could describe the situation of a sleeping person, a comatose patient, or a mentally challenged subject with regard to the capacity for intellectual knowledge.

This means that every person must be respected in the workplace and helps one to understand why all types of discrimination are negative and destructive for an organization. Even in things that would appear to be more minor, treating people differently or preferentially based on differences would cause problems—giving more information about work to those in the team who laugh at one's jokes; treating a colleague badly because he does not get the point quickly; not taking up other people's ideas or suggestions because one feels superior in intelligence; idolizing those members of staff who appear to always have smart solutions to issues, while not appreciating the contribution of the rest in other spheres of business activity; and many more.

## Knowledge and Truth

What is the object or purpose of knowledge? It is the truth. If the lecturer were to say to you "I saw Cecilia in the corridor as I was coming into the classroom," how would you know if he was telling the truth? You would want to know not about the logical or the grammatical correctness of what he said, but about the reality—did he see Cecilia in the corridor? Therefore, the question would be "Could he possibly have seen her?" If he is blind, you could already conclude that he did not in fact see Cecilia, because a real detail would have indicated to us the impossibility. You would want to find out if Cecilia was in the corridor at the time when she was "seen" there. And so, you would ask Cecilia—"Were you in such and such a corridor at such and such a time?" If she said to you that she was not, you would be left with two contradictory statements.

You might attempt to resolve this conflict based on the known credibility of both parties. If the lecturer is known never to tell the truth, you could dismiss his statement once Cecilia had contradicted it. If Cecilia is an inveterate liar, you could dismiss her statement and conclude that the lecturer did see her. However, in either case, the truth would be your standard. What is this truth? What you really want to know is what really happened. Did this man really see this lady in the corridor? And so, if both of them are known to you to be ordinarily truthful or ordinarily untruthful, you would seek an objective source of knowing the reality.

You could ask other people who may have been in the corridor if they saw Cecilia. You could look for evidence that Cecilia was elsewhere. You could, if there are security cameras, go through the videos to see if they caught Cecilia in the corridors. In every case, you would be looking for the reality, in order to be able to affirm that what the lecturer has said is true. Though it is not always such a tortuous process, when we seek to know, we ordinarily seek to know the truth, and we confirm the truth by reference to reality. The truth is not created in our minds. Even if I think that the market ought to operate in this manner, I cannot make it do so by thinking so. It is more useful for me to study the reality of the way the market operates and to learn the truth. If the actions of companies are affecting the planet, we cannot think it away or ignore it.

The reality exists outside of our minds, outside of us. Hence the importance of never compromising in seeking the truth of things and of events. Managers who go around blind, indifferent, or insensitive to the truth about what is going on around them later on get shocked at outcomes. When such insensitivity is exhibited toward the people who work with them, the resulting shock can be crippling or at least a substantial setback for the organization, because human beings are so unique and unpredictable that at least we need to acknowledge and respect this truth about them in order to know them and to lead them.

## Innovation and Creativity

There are job roles in which "creativity" is not reckoned with, where emphasis is placed not on lateral thinking but rather on logical sequential thinking and on being disciplined in following laid-down procedure. This latter style therefore contrasts with the liberal approach that prevails in roles in industries such as advertising and marketing. Whatever the case, a work environment in which employees are not allowed to use their minds by being innovative and creative in the way they work may eventually stifle them. At the very best, it will not optimize the resources the company has. Mansoor said that when he volunteered a suggestion in his office that he felt could improve the way things were done and bring greater profitability, he was shut up. Later on, the company paid millions to a consultant who recommended exactly what Mansoor had suggested. Mansoor did not stay long with the company, despite a fat compensation package and a prestigious role. He gradually became frustrated by the inability to use his intellect in the way he wanted.

Human beings act without having to be induced or manipulated when they see the point of doing so. For example, a company that wishes to embrace sustainability would do well to organize a forum to explain to the staff the reasons behind the policies the company wishes to adopt.

If the policies are simply driven top–down and the staff are not carried along, they may resist the change and this could be simply due to a lack of understanding. This idea is critical for managers who, at times, need to overcome a myopic perspective about the concept of motivation—believing that giving people material "incentives" is the only way to get them to do work, and therefore relying on operant conditioning. In fact, while this could work for animals, for children, and for adults who have been psychologically or physically reduced to an infrahuman state, it cannot be sustainably applied to fully grown human beings effectively.

## Layered Thinking

We are able to think in layers: we can think about what we are thinking about. We can think about the very act of thinking. We can make a judgment connecting the fact that we are thinking about what we are thinking to the concept of good or bad: "I should not be thinking…" And so we could go on and on. The fact is that, as Aristotle says in *Nicomachean Ethics*, "men have elegant minds." Human resources are for this very reason particularly special to organizations. Learning organizations are organizations that learn both from within and from without their walls. They are sensitive to the wealth of potential in the human resources they manage and are able to transform this into value for the organization and for the society.

Perhaps one could get used to staying on the surface because thinking requires effort. As lamented by Margaret Thatcher, in the film "*The Iron Lady*,"[3] one of the tragedies of our times is the emphasis on feeling rather than thinking. Also in the film, quoting her father she says that we are required to watch our thoughts because they become words; our words because they become actions; our actions because they become habits; our habits because they become our character; our character because it becomes our destiny, thereby emphasizing the primacy of thought over feeling. It is worth our while to make the effort and to resist any pressure from the environment that urges us to live at the level of feeling rather than of thought.[4]

The temptation to be superficial could be due to many varied reasons. One could be that we do not like what is revealed about ourselves when we think deeply. A boss who is appalled to hear that his subordinates consider him overbearing and stuffy would probably see it clearly if he spared some time for reflection. Hiding from the truth, like the proverbial ostrich, does not make it less true. Another source of temptation could be the temporary animal satisfaction that we can derive from allowing our emotions to override reason—venting anger, lust, greed, etc. We can deliberately refuse to be rational in order to gratify ourselves at a lower level, at times simultaneously denying that others may do the same, thus validating Oscar Wilde's humorous observation that man is a rational animal who always gets angry when asked to follow the dictates of reason. Since emotions are temporary, any fulfillment we get from giving way to them is also temporary, and therefore assuaging them cannot confer the more lasting fulfillment that is appropriate to a rational human nature.

## Education

*Knowing enough*: Intellectual knowledge, as opposed to sense knowledge, resides in the mind and uses the brain as a tool. The mind is not perfect, just as its owner is not perfect. Thus, sometimes it can be mistaken. We can err in our reasoning process and arrive at judgments that are contrary to the reality. This means that we need to constantly be interested in the truth of things. The truer our knowledge is, the better decisions we will make. Managers who are concerned to educate their minds before acting will spend the necessary time studying situations in order to avoid hasty and regrettable actions. They will seek to know the truth about events before judging them. Thus, for example, such a manager will take a second look when he sees a performance appraisal in which the supervisor's assessment is very far from the subordinate's, will listen to both sides when a report is made, will investigate customer complaints, etc.

Also, we do not know everything, and we can always learn more. Our mind has an infinite capacity for improvement. The awareness of these facts helps managers to be open to others' opinions and judgments and able to leverage on this to make optimal decisions. Besides, a manager who understands this is more likely to be committed to developing the capacity of his or her subordinates. It also enhances sensitivity to knowledge opportunities around us and readiness for change, such as a change in market dynamics, in economic variables, or in the competitive landscape.

For instance, now we know things about the planet that we did not know some years ago. Accepting our own limitations with regard to knowledge and being open to learn more about reality helps an organization to have a learning attitude and to be ready to change when there is a need to do so for the common good.

*Knowledge and the emotions*: the emotions can help us to know correctly and act well, as already mentioned in the previous chapter. A desire to become a doctor would help a young person to take his studies seriously and to follow a demanding schedule in order to pass his exams. However, emotions can also interfere with knowledge, either to cloud it or to prevent acting on it. We can look here at the case of someone who dislikes her boss. If she does not actively control this tendency, it could affect her ability to listen objectively to instructions from the boss and lead to bias whenever they interact, in such a way that this prevents her from seeing the truth when the boss in fact makes an effort to be nice and kind. Emotions can come in to lead the subordinate to interpret the boss's action always in a wrong manner and arrive at wrong conclusions that are not the truth. We could apply this also in the opposite direction—a boss who is carried away by anger with a subordinate will not easily be able to assimilate the truth about things concerning that person while the anger lasts.

Emotions can prevent a person from acting on knowledge, on truth. One implication of this is that organizations should accompany an appeal to the minds of their people with fostering the right emotions that would facilitate that people not only accept the truth presented to their minds but also overcome possible interference from negative emotions. For example, a polite request rather than a domineering command may make it easier for a subordinate to put his best into the task at hand. Educating the emotions and being able to control them help resolve the kind of situations that are envisaged in this paragraph and in the preceding one.

*Knowledge and the will*: following the same aforementioned example, when looking at our own experience and at people around us, we quickly realize that simply knowing is not enough. Even if one knows the truth of what one ought to do, one can choose to do the opposite. Perhaps a very simple and commonly experienced instance is when one plans to wake up at a certain time in the morning having thought of many good reasons to do so, sets the alarm clock, and then decides when the alarm clock rings that whatever happens, one is not going to get up at this moment—*"Yes, I know I ought to get up now so I won't be late for work, so Susan won't be left alone to face the client, so I can reply to Andrew's email and he can get on with his work (he's been waiting for it for four days) but what the heck, I'm not going to and I don't very much care what goes wrong because of it."* The person knows what to do but needs a strong enough will to overcome physical tiredness or emotional reluctance to do it. In such a situation, he may be helped by additional reasons (a reflection on the possible consequences for himself or his organization) or positive emotions (an appeal to his sense of duty, a reminder that one of the persons affected is a friend) etc. Thus, these two spiritual powers of knowing and doing (intellect and will) work as one to help the person to do good and to do well. This is why the next chapter focuses on the human will.

## Coffee Cues

People may not be fully satisfied with a job that engages only the animal functions. Without knowing the exact reason, they begin to feel vaguely restless, wanting to be more challenged, wanting to give an opinion, to express themselves, to use their own initiative. When in an environment in which this is not allowed, the person may feel stifled and find it difficult to remain there.

## Exercises and Project

Practice critiquing and countering your own thinking processes thus: state what you would do to solve a social problem in your country if you were in a position to do so; then challenge your own thinking as if you had just heard someone in that position say what you have said; now defend your points to the challenger—moderating your earlier statement whenever necessary to yield to a superior argument.

*(Continued)*

Start reading something new every day, even if it is five pages of a textbook from another discipline or a cultural publication, and reflect on it for a few minutes afterwards, trying to understand what new knowledge you have added to your intellect.

Practice thinking in concentric circles: think of a problem that you or someone you know has to solve. Think up a possible solution to the problem. Write it down. Reflect on it and think about how it affects people and if you have left anyone out in that solution. Expand the solution to include those people. Reflect on it again and see if your solution has captured the short-term and the long-term realities. Expand the solution to include both standpoints. Reflect on it to see if your solution would work in other environments with different cultures. Expand your solution to incorporate possible ways of implementing it respecting different cultures.

Narrate five experiences, yours or others', where the emotions caused knowledge and truth to be disregarded. Suggest how such conflicts could have been resolved.

# CHAPTER 5

# A Capacity for Good

This chapter is about how the human will follows human knowledge. As with the other chapters, it starts with an introduction to some concepts, followed by a case study, and then a discussion of the concepts with the case study and other illustrations.

Our will is attracted by whatever appears to us as good. Even when someone wants something that is bad for him, the reason for wanting it will be some good aspect of that thing, as, for example, the case of a person who drinks to forget. He knows that imbibing alcohol to excess is bad for him, but he wants the peace of oblivion. Since we are limited and cannot compass all possible goods, these goods must be ordered according to a hierarchy. No matter how much one wants it, one cannot sleep in two rooms at the same time.

Incidentally, the will or inclination of the person follows the intellect. When we perceive something as good, it is usually because our intellect has made a judgment that linked the notion "good" with that reality that we know. Hence, if we are mistaken, either in knowing the thing wrongly or mistakenly judging that it is good, our will will also be led astray in adhering to that thing to which we have erroneously attributed goodness.

## Case: The ChiaraPlus Scandal

### Part I

My name is Yolanda Harrison. I wish to narrate my experience in Megamania Bank.

I work in Megamania bank as an Account officer whose job function ranges from convincing prospects to deposit money with the bank to giving out loans to customers who need loans to run their businesses.

The bank has a credit facility—Authority to Load Facility—for oil traders who cannot play in the major oil market. The transaction dynamics of this facility after approval by the bank's management team are as follows:

**Step 1:** The bank disburses the amount requested by the customer into the customer's account; however, the customer does not have direct access to the funds.

**Step 2:** The customer submits a proposal specifying a product (diesel, kerosene, or fuel) that he or she wants to buy, stating the amount of the product, the quantity, and the name of the supplier.

**Step 3:** The bank raises a manager's check (MC) to the tune of the amount of the product cost, in favor of the supplier.

**Step 4:** An account officer, representing the bank and working with the customer, takes the check to the suppliers' office and exchanges it for Authority-to-Load cards. This is done because the suppliers usually have tank farms where products are stored and the trading customer, who cannot afford a tank farm, leaves the product in the supplier's tank and only goes to take the product whenever he has buyers. The bank requests these cards because they want to know when the customer collects some product from the supplier and sells it, in order to know when to collect the proceeds from him. Before the customer goes to the supplier to collect the product or part of it, the bank officer signs off on the Authority-to-Load card. This is simultaneously a permission card for the supplier to allow the trader to take the product out of the tank and an instrument for monitoring the transaction by the bank.

Last week, I had to attend to this customer (ChiaraPlus) who, unknown to me, had already planned with its supplier (Everfuel) to divert the bank's money. Or, at least, that is what I think is going on. The relieving account officer (the main account officer) is on leave; this is why I was asked to handle the deal. The Managing Director of Chiara-Plus brought the proposal herself (Step 2). Since it had been approved, I raised the MC (Step 3) and wanted to take it to the supplier to exchange for the Authority-to-Load card (Step 4) according to the bank's policy.

My manager, Mr. Mark, asked me to give the MC to ChiaraPlus instead of Everfuel. I politely declined to follow his instructions, though I was quaking with fear inside, and reminded him of the bank's policy. He disagreed with me, insisting that I should do as I had been told. He said he would sign off to exonerate me in case "issues" arose in future. I told him, again politely, that I was only trying to save his neck and mine.

At that point, he stopped the conversation because we were in the presence of other staff members. I am afraid that he will ask me again, or that he will victimize me if I refuse again. I have heard stories of employees who have been terminated or lived a miserable life because of their bosses.

My colleagues do not see why I am disobeying my boss. After all, he has said that he will sign off on the handover document. The customer is furious and has been calling me names. She says that her former account officer was always in her favor. She could file a spurious complaint against me to the customer service department. It would be my word against hers if I explain what really happened, especially since my boss would not support me. I do not have anyone to turn to for advice. I do not want to lose my job. I just got it last month and my employment has not yet been confirmed.

## Part II

I decided to be faithful to my convictions and stand firm. However, because I did not give Madam ChiaraPlus the opportunity to execute her diversion plans, she stopped the transaction halfway and waited for her usual account officer to resume. When Carla, the account officer, resumed from leave, I gave her a report on what I had done so far on the transaction. I also told her my suspicions and my reasons for not doing what the customer had requested. She said she understood. I later discovered that the transaction was executed immediately and that she carried out the wishes of the customer to the letter and gave the MC to the lady directly rather than to the supplier. This meant that the customer now had access to the funds directly. Carla definitely went against the bank's policy. I do not know what to do about it. I really do not want to get into trouble. I have no idea who else is in on this within the bank.

*Epilogue*

Unknown to me, the branch manager, the account officer, and the customer were all in on the deal. They shared the loan money among the three of them. I never did get to know in what proportions. However, after some months, the bank expected the customer to pay back and she could not. Then my manager and the account officer were suspended on the condition that they would be recalled after they recovered the money from the customer. Neither of them could face the customer to ask for the money because they had compromised their values.

## Coffee Quiz

1. Why did Yolanda and Carla disagree?
2. What helped Yolanda to stand firm?

## Purpose and Choice

At different crossroads in life, some more important and others less, we constantly make choices about what to do. When we know something, we are able to make some judgment as to whether it is good or bad. After we make that judgment, our will is attracted to the thing if it is good, and repelled if it is bad. We commonly express this with the words "want" and "not wanting." For example, if I read about sunny weather on the beach in Miami, it is likely to register on my intellect as something good and therefore simultaneously attract my will. If I, on the other hand, hear that my neighbors were attacked in the night by armed robbers, it is likely to register on my intellect as something bad and repel my will. It is something I do not want.

Aristotle explained that the good things that attract us vary in their nature.[1] Some are activities, such as studying, and others result from activities, for example, passing the exam. Some are good in themselves, such as knowledge, while others are good because they help us to attain those that are good in themselves, for example, money. They can be ordered in a pyramidal model representing a hierarchy of goods, where those goods that we seek for their own sake are higher than those we seek as instruments to attain the former. Those that are higher are more worthy of our attention and give us humans more chance of fulfillment, especially since they tend to be more intangible than the instrumental goods and also more social in the sense that they do not place us in competition with each other to attain them. While one man having more money might reduce the amount of money available to another, one having more knowledge does not in any way disturb its acquisition by others. Given this hierarchy, if a person seeks a good that is instrumental in a way that harms the chance of attaining higher goods, then it is bad for the person.

The distinction between good and bad is not always so clear. Many decisions are good in one sense and bad in another. Therefore, some managerial issues need to be studied in depth in order to take decisions that are really and truly good. To determine what is truly good, we need to again look for the truth in reality. And the reality of what is good for man will be found in what is good not only subjectively but also objectively. Thus, for example, the way to treat people—customers, employees, creditors, and suppliers—should always respect their dignity and the ensuing rights—the right to consideration, the right not to be harmed, the right to fair hearing, the right to privacy, etc. Actions that debase human nature are bad for the actor who is going against his own nature by acting against human nature; they are bad for those affected by the act, whose rights have been disregarded or violated, and they are bad for the common good of mankind, and all these whether or not the people involved are aware of what is going on. Nothing can make this kind of action good—not doing it with a good intention, not considering some good consequences that could result from it. Attesting to this, Pope John Paul II said: "The rational ordering of the human act to the good in its truth and the voluntary pursuit of that good, known by reason, constitute morality. Hence, human activity cannot be judged as morally good merely because it is a means for attaining one or another of its goals, or simply because the subject's intention is good."[2]

Thus, for example, if an organization were to lay off staff without reason, without consideration, and without a fair process, they would have disregarded the right of those people to a fair and respectful treatment and thus the action would be bad. It would be bad even if the intention behind it was to accrue some value to the shareholders, which is a good intention, and it would be bad even if it had the consequences of accruing that value or of facilitating a pay rise for those staff left behind. This does not mean that a company cannot disengage staff, but that it should not be done irrationally, inconsiderately, or unfairly. Similarly, a member of staff can resign from a company, with reason, with due considerateness, and being fair to the people he is leaving behind.

Besides, just as the intellect is not perfect and could be deformed, so could the will. An untrained will can lead the owner to consistently carry out actions that he knows are bad for him and omit actions that would have been beneficial to him. It is for this reason that it is universally acknowledged that it is important to grow in willpower—educate the will in order to be able to hold on to what is good even when it is difficult to achieve, and resist what is bad even when it seems easy to do and presents some good aspects.

## Education

In order to be able to demonstrate a firm will in moments of great temptation to do the opposite of what one really considers to be right, it is useful to habitually exercise the will in order to educate it. A business owner or a highly placed manager might need to make a choice to report less profit and to instead raise the salaries of the underpaid workers in the organization or to spend some money on waste management so as to avoid polluting a nearby stream. If he is used to making decisions that go against his pleasure, it will be easier for him than if he has never denied himself any whim. Similarly, an employee may be greatly tempted to spend time surfing the net during work hours if no one can see what he is doing at his desk. Yet, he may know that the pile of work on the desk is really what should take priority.

Denying oneself in things that are legitimate is sometimes referred to as building up willpower, so that one will be able to count on that "reservoir" of willpower in moments when it is really needed. Others call it the development of self-mastery. Whatever the terminology, the learning point is that a will thus educated will find it easier to apply itself to the work at hand and desist from the enjoyment of a lesser though attractive good, and will find it easier also to refrain from acts that harm others or harm the environment.

## Determination

When someone is able to hold firm by displaying willpower from the beginning of a project to the end, we say that the person is determined. This is an attribute that is very much needed in the world of work, where difficulties could discourage one from going ahead. An entrepreneur who is not determined may easily give up and fold up his firm when problems arise. Succeeding in a career usually demands determination—working against the odds, not giving up when things are tough, etc. When someone is determined that the new IT equipment acquired by the organization will work, the effort he will put into ensuring that it does will probably greater than if he were the kind of person who is easily discouraged.

One of the areas in which determination helps in working well with others is in controlling the signs of liking or disliking. Liking or disliking is usually irrational, one of those things that happen to people, based on natural traits—unsuited temperaments, different senses of humor, different ways of manifesting emotions, etc.—something that is difficult to explain could just make one person dislike another without actually having any known reason to do so. If the two people find themselves assigned to the same task in the workplace, they would need to overcome the dislike (whether unilateral or mutual) in order to be able to give their best in the assignment entrusted to them by the firm. A determined effort not to show such like or dislike will go a long way in overcoming it either temporarily or permanently. This type of determination is also required of managers so that they are able to treat their staff fairly and not discriminate among them based on liking or disliking. Any perception of preferential treatment can easily lead to people feeling badly dealt with and can harm their sense of loyalty to their boss and or to the firm.

Determination helps us to achieve the purpose of the will when it loves.[3] When the will adheres firmly to a good, this is called love and it is based on the person's rationality and not on feeling. Thus, it is that one might, despite preferring to stay at home, spend the evening accompanying a spouse who wished to go out; or one might listen to a friend who is being utterly boring; or do one's work even if there are a hundred things one would prefer to be doing instead and which would be more pleasurable as far as feeling is concerned. Love that is understood and experienced only as a feeling could not last, since feeling, no matter how long its duration, is still tied to the body and is therefore temporary. Only love that inheres in the spiritual will can last, sharing in the indestructibility of the will.

## Locus of Control

People who blame what happens to them—their own actions and events that befall them—on causes external to themselves are said to have an external locus of control. They do not see what they could have done to prevent those things. In this way, they abdicate control of their own lives. Research shows that people who have a high internal locus of control—who take the responsibility for their actions and for the events of their lives—are more likely to succeed in competitive environments than those who do not. One of the reasons for this is that someone who looks inwards rather than playing the blame game is more likely to discover what to improve in and therefore to take whatever decisions are necessary to make progress.

## Leadership

The essential traits of a leader include having clarity of vision, a sense of mission, courage and willpower, self-knowledge, humility, and a sense of responsibility. Apart from knowing and communicating where he is leading people to, the person who wishes to lead needs to know and accept his strengths and weaknesses in order to maximize his strengths and find ways to overcome or supplement his weaknesses. He also needs to be able to stand firm in the face of difficulties and to encourage those who are following him. In addition, he needs to hold himself accountable to his followers and to the wider society who have entrusted him with the mantle of leadership.

As we saw earlier, the fact of knowing something does not always make it easy to do it. Therefore, a strong will, the power to act on what one knows, is also needed to lead oneself and to lead others. When a leader allows his will to be weakened by emotions and passions, he easily ends up acting irresponsibly and lacking the qualities required for leadership, as can be seen, for example, in the instances of greed revealed in the ethical scandals that occasionally hit the headlines. However, such weakening of the will usually will not have happened overnight. Business, in order to be a responsible member of society, needs to train leaders rightly and to tighten the controls that help to detect early when deviations start.

## Coffee Cues

Yolanda's knowledge of the transaction dynamics enabled her to realize what was going on. Otherwise she could have done the wrong
thing just following the customer's instructions. But knowledge was
not enough; she needed to act on that knowledge by doing what she
believed to be right in spite of the obstacles. Yolanda exercised her freedom to resist her manager's request though it was not easy for her. She
made a difficult choice not to go against the bank's policy even though
she knew that her manager would not be happy with her decision
and that he could use it against her, for example, during the periodic
appraisal exercise or in an accusation of insubordination.

After thinking it over, she decided that she did not want to com-
promise her values and was ready to take responsibility for her actions.
She had tried to give her manager and Carla reasons why they should
also abide by the bank's policy. They did not. Many other staff of the
bank engaged in the same unethical practice and the bank eventually
collapsed.

What helped Yolanda to stand firm? She kept remembering that
the whole essence of insisting that the borrowing customer pays back is
because the funds given to them belong to other people who deposited
their money with the bank for safekeeping. In this case, Yolanda did
succeed in leading herself; despite her fears, she was able to do what
she really wanted to do, to abide by the bank's policy. She was, however, not able to lead those around her, perhaps because of her newness
within that work environment.

A number of employees of Megamania bank who were involved in
unethical behavior said that they did what they did because everyone
else did the same. Others said that it was because the temptation was
too great, that the bank should have had tighter controls. Yet others
simply blamed their bosses and the customers who put pressure on
them. In each of the above, an external locus of control is reflected.
This is a barrier to leadership ability and the development of a sense of
responsibility. As much as possible, and without overdoing it, a mod-
erately high internality should be cultivated in order to be able to lead
oneself and others.

## Exercises and Project

Do a minute paper. Answer three questions (printed out on individual sheets or projected on a screen) in the last minute of the class:

1. What has been your most interesting discovery so far?
2. What have you found most useful for practical application?
3. What is your most burning unanswered question so far?

Select two positive habits that you would like to develop but have found difficult so far. Break each down into the actions that are required and begin to put in more effort to carry out those actions. For example, someone who wishes to be punctual might identify stopping current activities 5 minutes before the next one as an action. Similarly, someone who wishes to be kind might identify smiling at a colleague as one of the actions that make up kindness. Another may wish to be tidier and may identify putting back each work tool in the place it was picked up from as one of the actions.

Use Rotter's instrument[4] or one adapted from it to assess your locus of control. Suggest steps that could increase the internality of one's locus of control. Also suggest steps to take to mitigate an internal locus of control that is too strong.

# CHAPTER 6

# Integration in Complexity

Despite the detailed discussion of different aspects and characteristics of man so far, it is important to remind oneself that man is not a composite as such. He is one. All those parts are so united that it is impossible to delineate them. For example, a division cannot be clearly drawn to determine whether it is the spiritual part of man that is acting or the material; whether it is the emotions that are solely involved in a reaction or the will, where the intellect stops and the will takes over, etc.

Understanding the unity of the elements that make up man and the diversity of operations of these elements helps one to personally take responsibility for all of one's actions or inaction rather than shift blame. From a managerial perspective, it helps one appreciate that in the course of performing professional and official duties, the state of an employee's mind has a bearing on the physical actions and vice versa, with the implication being that one should go out of one's way to show concern for the personal lives of the people with whom one works.

Neglecting either of the two aspects of a human being leads to an erroneous understanding of who he is and of how to relate with him. For example, carrot and stick approaches to management mimic operant conditioning, which, as already said, is inadequate for adult humans.[1] Neglecting the emotional side of people could also have negative consequences, as depicted in the film "The Chorus," where orphans are transformed and given a purpose by a new teacher who cares for them.[2]

## Case: Martine Ferrer

Martine Ferrer worked at Trusted Mortgage Bank. She had been working as a marketer at the bank for 5 years and had received many commendations on her output. She enjoyed her work and had made many friends among her colleagues because of her sunny personality. Even their usually dour boss often unbent towards her.

Her duties included the writing of a report based on daily activities. On one Tuesday afternoon, she was having strong dysmenorrheal pains and could not concentrate on her work. In addition, she was rather upset because a client she had visited earlier in the day made amorous advances towards her. It angered her and she managed to put him off, yet she was worried about how to manage the situation because the bank needed the client's account.

She had returned to the office after a long day of marketing and was now trying to prepare the report based on the day's activities. Due to some degree of distraction, she made a number of mistakes she would not have ordinarily made. For example, she wrote "the" instead of "their" in a sentence where it actually distorted the overall sense.

When her boss read through the memo, he noticed the errors. He was furious and started shouting at her; he ended by flinging the report at her in the presence of a superior boss and her subordinates. Martine could not do any meaningful work for the rest of the week. She kept thinking of how she had been treated and continued feeling miserable. Her boss also remained angry with her for the rest of the week and would at times pick on her without obvious cause. Her 5-year historically brilliant performance seemed to count for nothing now. She began to consider resigning from the bank before she was sent out. She did not have many alternatives, but she did not enjoy her work any longer and just wanted to get out of Trusted Mortgage Bank.

## Coffee Quiz

1. Why was Martine affected by her boss's reactions?
2. Advise Martine: should she resign?

## One Single Me

Despite all the components we seem to have broken human nature into in the preceding chapters, it is very important to retain our awareness that each one of us is one whole being. We are not a conglomerate of organs, will, emotions, limbs, intellect, instincts, and senses trying to work together. Each person is simply a person, and there is no way to totally isolate any of these elements that make up each individual as a separate entity. The whole person is the one who acts. A mother who gets up in the night to attend to her crying baby is acting based on instinct, feeling, and intelligent love at the same time, and it would be impossible to draw clear distinctions between these as if they were separate components of her action. This idea, basic as it may seem, has some consequences for understanding ourselves and for understanding others.

As a lecturer at an Executive MBA program[3] once explained: if some-one were to slap you, and say to you, "Oh so sorry, that was not me; it was my hand that slapped you," you would think he was a joker or a lunatic. Either way, it would be an impossible statement. The person is the one who has done the slapping. In the same way, if my stomach has a problem and I suffer from indigestion, the whole me has the problem. Thus, it may affect my mood that day, making me irritable in the office. It may affect my work pace or even work quality, since I may not be able to concentrate as fully as usual. It may affect the speed with which I would ordinarily think and assimilate ideas, etc. It may also affect my willingness to be nice to others that day. I may see that my colleague is having challenges handling a difficult customer, and I may choose to remain wrapped up in my problem of indigestion rather than help out. Whatever happens to the body happens to the person and may actually be manifested by its effects on the emotions, on the mind, on the will, etc.

Similarly, if I am finding it difficult to understand some intellectual problem, my mind concentrates and my brow furrows without my actu-ally taking a decision to carry my body along. This is the unity of the mind and body, described rather humorously by Terry Pratchett in *Thief of Time*[4] as the body having a mind of its own. Lady LeJean's shoulder lifts in a shrug without her expecting it or planning to; she has not been used to a body and does not understand why it is acting thus. David's smile, in *I am David*[5] comes spontaneously when for the first time he is happy— the corners of his mouth lift up and behold, he is smiling for the first time in his life. Before that, he had tried to and he could not, no matter how much he contorted his face.

Because we are different, the extent and the manner of these inter-actions also differ. One person may be able to continue working with a headache; another person may not. One person may be able to smile at everyone in the office even after a series of sleepless nights; another may find it very difficult and may go around somewhat grouchy. Each person needs to know his own tendencies in order to recognize and acknowledge what is happening to him *("I don't know why I feel so down in the dumps")* and in order to make sure that it does not mar the quality of his interactions with others insofar as possible. (If you quarrel with a client today because you had bad news or a bad dinner or a disagreement with your husband the previous day, you will only create for yourself the extra work needed to repair that relationship in future, if it is not irrevocably damaged).

Each person also needs to understand that, at times, there is something else influencing the behavior of others towards him and so be able to make excuses for them and see beyond what is manifested at that moment. If my boss does not ordinarily snap at me, then perhaps he is snapping today because he stubbed his big toe on his way into the building, because he was given a parking ticket when he drove out to lunch, because his fiancée has broken up with him, because his own boss snapped at him, or a host of other possible reasons that have nothing to do with me. Of course, none of these things give him an excuse to snap at me. They are simply possible reasons for the action, and realizing their possible existence could help me to overlook the snapping and not react in a way that damages the relationship between my boss and me.

The way in which we treat one another should also take into consideration these components. An organization that provides training for its employees and pays them well may still lose their full commitment simply because it fails to provide convenient access to drinking water and food, perhaps by providing water dispensers and establishing cafeteria services or outsourcing the provision of meals to those interested. As the adage goes, a hungry man (and a thirsty one too perhaps) is an angry man. Surely a company full of angry men has a problem or will soon develop one.

When managing subordinates, at times, one can intuit that something must be causing the poor performance of that guy—a personal relationship gone sour, problems with the children, a recent bereavement, challenges with finding accommodation or paying the rental, etc. and perhaps simply showing some understanding could help the person begin to get over the problem. Being able to sense things like this and give the person space or consideration or whatever is needed is part of emotional intelligence. For the organizations that consciously practice or foster it, empathy goes a long way in helping to bring people together to work as a team towards the company's goals. This is because such a culture helps people to see that they are not considered as mere resources such as tables or chairs but as human beings, with all that is consequent on possessing human nature.

## Personality and Character

We forge our character and build our personality by exerting the intelligence and the will to bring harmony into our whole being. This is where nature and nurture stop to give way to the exercise of freedom. We shall discuss freedom and the development of character more fully in Chapters 11 and 12. Suffice it here to simply mention that all the above influences have roles to play.

## Integrity and Unity of Life

True, a human being is first an animal, and therefore he has some natural tendencies (instincts) and basic needs. However, he does not always have to succumb to these instincts, or to the strongest of them, as would happen with the lower animals. He is set apart by the ability to choose—to bring intelligence and will to know the truth and choose the good.

The difference between man and other animals therefore lies in a "spiritual essence." There is that part of the human being that is incorruptible because it is not made up of material parts and therefore transcends the material world. Yet he is a single being, and not a spirit driving a body or a body animated by a spirit. When a human being acts with this wholeness, he is said to have integrity.

There is a need to educate one's emotions in order to increase the ability to choose one's reactions. Reactions do not have to be always spontaneous; one can choose to pause and think before reacting. Similarly, it is important to educate the intellect, in order to fill it with more truth and enable it to make truer judgments, and to educate the will by strengthening it to respect the hierarchy of goods. This effort is the process of forging one's personality and character, and it takes time. Over that time, what happens is that the person practices habits. The repetition of actions by man leads to a disposition towards that action, which has now become habitual. If the habit is good, then the disposition to do it is a virtue and contributes to developing the person. When it is bad, it is a vice and harms the person. To develop oneself therefore and enhance one's dispositions to do good by default, one must first identify which habits to change, and the habits to replace them with. Chapter 12 discusses this further.

In addition, man cannot succeed, or be happy or fulfilled, alone. This will be discussed in Chapter 8. He must seek the good of others in order to achieve his own good. This is why people often resolve to put their family first. Whether they succeed in doing so is another matter.

Many take for granted the marked differences between human beings and animals, being merely content with the clichéd position that human beings are a higher version of animals. An ability to appreciate those unique factors that set man on a higher pedestal in comparison to even the "highest" of animals makes us more demanding of excellence from ourselves and from those we work with. It makes one seek to act as a human being, rationally,[6] in all situations and therefore achieve a consistency that enhances integrity. One would then seek to be one's best self not only at work but also at home (and vice versa), and one would be conscious of and respect others' way of being not only at work but also at home, in social life, etc.

## Living and Acting in the Present

The memory and the imagination at times push us to stay out of our present reality and get caught up in the past and in the future respectively. When this happens, it may be difficult to give due concentration to one's work or other present engagements and this can easily lead to suboptimal performance and to misunderstandings and conflicts at work. To avoid wasting time lamenting or reliving the past that has gone by or anticipating or dreading a future that may never come, willpower can be exercised to direct one's thoughts to the present each time the past or the future threaten to take over. Thus, one will tend more and more to live in the present, which in any case is the only time in which one can truly live. It also frees up the person more to engage better with others—letting go of past misunderstandings and future possible conflicts in order to work together on achieving whatever is presently entrusted to the team.

It could happen that a person seeks to drown memories in alcohol or drugs. This is not an ideal solution to the intrusion of memory into the present, and it does more harm than good since it harms the human body and can end up incapacitating its reasoning ability. When one needs to deliberately strive to forget matters that take up present energy without adding value, such as going over past failures or hurts to lament them,[7] there are healthier ways to do it. To manage such memories that are not helpful, one can develop the willpower to resist focusing on them and to move on to other things.[8]

## Coffee Cues

Knowing our human nature well helps us to know our normal body rhythms and moods and how certain things affect us. Thus, we can brace for expected events and also assimilate well those that were unexpected, drawing on strong emotional reserves and willpower. A manager who knows that he is always irritated on Monday mornings will prepare himself to resist that tendency on those days so that it does not interfere with his performance or his relationship with his staff. Both Martine and her boss should take their emotionality into consideration and rationally moderate their reactions accordingly.

## Exercises

Try to make a conscious effort to live the present moment fully for the next couple of hours. In your next class session, do the same. Focus only on the session. Do not worry about whether you did well in yesterday's test or whether you brought enough lunch tickets to school, or whether you should not have shouted at the gateman when you left

*(Continued)*

*(Continued)*

the house. Do not worry about what the next lecturer will say when she discovers that you did not read the case study, or whether the car will start, or whether it will rain tomorrow when you are driving from the island to the mainland. These are things you cannot do anything about while the session is going on. Do not try to rehearse what you will say to your aunt when she calls or to enjoy in advance the beautiful ice cream that your roommate put in the deep freezer. These are things that will only take away from your present concentration, and from experience, you know that the reality will probably be different from what you can imagine.

Imagine that a man and a monkey are locked up for two days in two adjacent rooms, without food or water. At the end of the period, a ripe bunch of bananas is placed on a stool in front of the monkey's door and a plate of appetizing food is placed on a stool in front of the man's door. What do you think would happen if both doors were opened? What would be the possible reasons behind what you think would happen? Would there be a difference if the period was longer? Please give a reason for your response to this last question.

# MODULE 2

# Working with Others

# CHAPTER 7

# Diversity and Uniqueness

## Diversity

Each human being is different; this is a reality that one needs to consciously accept and learn to cope with. Given so many differences in genetic makeup, temperament, cultural, social, and physical environment, education, and experience, it is surely not surprising that each one of us turns out so differently. Add to these the tendencies consolidated and the habits built by our free choices, and it becomes clear that diversity is a factor to be reckoned with in any enterprise where people have gathered together to strive to achieve a common goal. Nature, nurture, and the use of freedom interact to make each one what he is and different from the others around him even in the case of identical twins brought up together and exposed to the same environment.

Diversity leads to different ways of seeing things and therefore different ways of approaching projects, solving problems, etc. A person who is not conscious of this diversity would easily constitute a problem for the organization because he would constantly be making plans assuming that everyone thinks like him and agrees with him. Sensitivity to diversity implies being open to others and ready to accept that they have views and opinions that may be as valid as one's own until proven otherwise and so need to be taken into account. And so, for example, a manager may think that the best color to paint the walls of a factory is green. However, he may discover when the staff who are actually going to work in the factory are asked, that they would prefer the walls to be beige.

The diversity of humanity is a source of enrichment to organizations. It means that they can benefit from the innovations sparked by having unlike minds rub against one another and propose multiple answers to whatever challenge faces them. Everybody has something to offer, even the least in the organization as far as hierarchical status is concerned.

A cleaner could be the one to resolve a puzzle that the CEO could not tackle, drawing from a different experience well.

## Uniqueness

Due to the characteristic of interiority that belongs to persons as individuals, each person has his own ideas, inclinations, emotions, temperament, and physical capabilities, in short, his own personality, and together with all of these a history of choices that has left a mark on him. This makes each one of us unrepeatable and unique. Hence, it is irrational to allow oneself to get irritated when someone thinks differently or sees life differently or has a different sense of humor or a different sense of fashion. Human beings are not ciphers in an organization. In managing human resources, looking at job fit and individual plans for development are a good way to respect this uniqueness of the person.

In theories of motivation, this is also taken into consideration. What motivates one person may not motivate another. And the organization cannot probably afford to motivate some and rest on its laurels. Each person counts. Human nature is common to all of us and makes each human being in the end the same—with equal dignity and the same human rights, etc.

## Case: Aleksandra's Boss

I once had a job that I enjoyed dearly. I took up the opportunity not because of monetary gain but because I enjoy helping people be in harmony with God and live healthily. I lived on the island while my office was situated on the mainland.[1] This required me to stay with a friend on the mainland during the week and spend the weekends on the island.

As an administrative staff, I enjoyed working with my boss and everything went well, until it became evident that the only way I could move on with the job was to move in with her at her Magodo[2] residence. She never asked me if I would like to live with her; she was just acting as if I had agreed to do so, and I refused to be manipulated. She would make me close late by asking me to do things that were not urgent or to handle responsibilities that ordinarily were not within my jurisdiction to ensure I closed late and spent the night in her house. She also asked those staying with her to move out, assuming that I would be more comfortable in their absence. One would have expected me to jump at the idea but I could not because it would hinder some other things I would want to do and I did not want to be micromanaged. I had a work life and a personal life and I did not want their mixing together, one eliminating the other or one acting as the two.

What my boss wanted was not out of the ordinary; all she needed to make me comply was to give me reasons to accept her offer and help me experience the positive emotions of living with her. Probably, I would have explained my position on the matter and we could have struck a deal midway.

## Coffee Quiz

1. What do you think about Aleksandra's boss?
2. Have you ever experienced difficulty in explaining a difference of opinion to a close friend?

## Unrepeatability

Each human being is unique and unrepeatable. Appreciation of this makes it easier to work together in harmony because one learns to read each person differently and accept him as he is: some catch jokes more readily, some catch explanations more easily, some are more intuitive to what customers would like, etc.

At times, we expect other people to see things in exactly the same way as we do and then we are surprised that they do not, that in fact they have a totally different point of view. In learning to communicate effectively, this is sometimes described as the need to take into account that the person receiving one's message has a different frame of reference and so one should expect that the message sent from one's frame of reference will be decoded and re-encoded with a different frame that the other person has built up over the years. As each individual is so very different from the other, far from being surprised at the differences, we should see them as opportunities to learn from one another and to combine our unique characteristics and abilities in order to achieve even more.

# Openness

It is important, therefore, not to take things merely at surface value, but to always pause to think about why human beings act or react in the way they do, rather than being hasty to arrive at conclusions or make judgments. A tendency to think we already know can make us ascribe our own thinking patterns, motivations, etc. to others, and this would in many cases lead to wrong conclusions and perhaps to avoidable misunderstandings and conflicts.

One of the outcomes of a real appreciation for diversity is an environment where people feel safe, understood, and protected, and therefore are more likely to be committed to organizational goals and to go out of their way to do things that benefit the organization (sometimes referred to as organizational citizenship behavior). Since they are used to being heard, they bring up ideas freely knowing that their opinion will be heard and valued. They are more likely to live up to the dignity with which the company regards them. Rather than harbor resentments and vengeful feelings when injustice is perceived, they speak up and clear the air.

Going all out to leverage diversity is another stage. This entails consciously seeking the benefits of diversity rather than simply having social inclusion as a goal in itself. An organization that deliberately tries to harness and make the most of the diversity of its employees is more likely to benefit from that diversity than one that simply waits for it to happen by chance. This is why some organizations when constituting project teams put in a special effort to ensure that the group is heterogeneous.

A very good example of potential gains from diversity is the case of gender differences. Having men and women on a Board of Directors could lead to benefiting from differing and complementary perspectives and contributions during their deliberations; for example, the women might demonstrate greater perception, intuition, and attention to detail, while the men might display less risk-aversion and in general strengthen the decisiveness of the board.

In the film called *A Small Act*,[3] there is a scene where a committee meets to decide on which students from a rural community should be given a scholarship for secondary education. The students selected, based on academic performance, were boys. The committee appeared to have finished their job. However, the only woman in the team then commented on the need to educate girls also if they were to achieve their real aim of reducing poverty and enhancing development in that rural community. She also pointed out that the girls ordinarily had to start working with their mothers very early, and so could not dedicate as much time to study as the boys, and therefore perhaps different yardsticks would be needed to measure their academic potential. She also made the others see the importance of the role of the women of the community, who were the ones in charge of running the homes and bringing up the children, who would be the future leaders of the community, with the right values. Appreciating her reasoning, the committee reviewed its decisions and awarded more scholarships than originally planned, to include a couple of girls. This decision was to later have a very large impact on the community.

Nevertheless, in some organizations, there are still remnants of a lack of appreciation for diversity. This could be displayed in gender-biased succession planning, lack of patience with people who learn certain types of skills at a slower rate than others, recruitment that is biased against or in favor of particular ethnic or racial groups, etc. At the root of these kinds of incidences is a lack of understanding of the unicity and diversity of human nature.

### Tolerance

In many organizations, there are policies that foster diversity. For example, in order to promote and ensure that diversity is accepted, some companies consciously foster a mix of genders, ages, races, and cultural backgrounds in their recruitment process. In this way, they ensure that they practice social inclusion and not just avoid discrimination against people based on any of these accidental attributes. The substance remains the same—a human being who has the same dignity as any other and so deserves equal respect.

Beyond tolerance is empathy—the ability to put oneself in another's shoes. This is a skill that is important in managing people, because it makes it possible to understand others and therefore easier to help them to overcome obstacles, whether personal or professional, and be able to perform better at whatever personal, professional, or organizational goals they set themselves.

## Communication

Awareness of diversity helps one to communicate more effectively. In drafting a policy or a memo to staff, for example, one would be conscious of expressing the content not only in a way that makes sense to oneself but in a way that would make sense to all the other people who would read the document. In addition to clarity, one would also seek to edit out any aspect of the communication that could wound others' sensitivities.

### Coffee Cues

Aleksandra's boss assumed that she and her employee would see things exactly the same way. She did not trouble to explain. Assumptions can be dangerous. Aleksandra seems to have also made some assumptions, perhaps without realizing it.

### Exercises

Read the following anecdote: a young executive was leaving the office at 6 pm when he found the Managing Director standing in front of a shredder with a piece of paper in his hand. "Listen," said the Managing Director, "this is a very sensitive and important document and my secretary has left. Can you make this thing work?" "Certainly, Sir" said the young executive. He turned the machine on, inserted the paper, and pressed the start button. "Excellent, excellent!" said the Managing Director as his paper disappeared inside the machine. "I just need one copy." What are the underlying assumptions made by the protagonists?

During the rest of the week, check whether you listen to others' opinions or contributions in class with adequate respect for their right to be different.

# CHAPTER 8

# All Around the Manager

Human nature is essentially social. A person who is used to working in a small family business where interpersonal relationships are warm and relatively informal might find it difficult to adjust if he moves to a multinational corporation where the norm is "arms-length" relationships. Such a person is likely to highly value the close relationships developed over the years and may not be as comfortable with an impersonal work setting.

## Case: My Three Managers

My first manager, Stephen, understood people and used his insight to the company's advantage and ours. I had applied to be a Graduate Trainee, and on the day I was called to pick up my letter of appointment, he held a meeting with all the new Graduate Trainees during which he sold the organization to us. He shared his own experiences and told us how working in the organization would help us to grow in our areas of interest. He passed on to us the vision of the organization, and enthused us with the idea of working together to bring to fruition something that was bigger than ourselves. He also sold to us the joys of working in an organization that had community values. I must say that his pitch worked. We all responded to this man who seemed to believe we had a choice as to whether or not we wanted to work with him. I like to think that we were transformed during that meeting into a loyal and committed team, and from the beginning we were convinced that we had to work hard to build our competence, so that we would not fail him or the company. We had to deliver good service. Suddenly, we were a group of motivated young people with a common and lofty goal. Graduate Trainee salaries were not very high, but we were excited about coming to work each day, and about going the extra mile to achieve our vision.

He stayed with us for 6 months. During this period, he would make us write detailed weekly reports on what we had learnt so far, and what our high points and low points were. He always knew what challenges any of us had. No matter how busy he was, and whether he was in or outside the country or not, he would read our reports himself and reply with comments or suggestions to resolve the issues or answer our questions. He made himself accessible; we could go to talk to him about anything. He made a lot of cold calls on us and was always looking for feedback.

I used to wonder how he had the time for it all, but now, after my third manager, Charles, I understand why Stephen placed getting feedback as a top priority. Stephen understood that man is an emotional being. If I was having problems, this might affect my work negatively, and so he tried to deal with the problems that he could help with, so that we could be more productive. He even used to tell us that being emotionally intelligent is the key to becoming successful, but the full import of that statement was not clear to me then.

After 6 months, Stephen moved on to another department and we got a new manager. This new manager, Sharon, seemed to labor under the impression that we all were unintelligent. In addition, she never gave anybody credit for good work done. It was as if she thought the things got done miraculously by themselves, except when she was able to take the credit, and that seemed to be often, no matter who had been the actual protagonist. She found fault incessantly and exaggerated people's shortcomings. She presented herself as a perfectionist, who was trying to raise our standards, but she ended up demoralizing the team. After a while, people stopped trying to be creative or to make decisions on their own, because everything was received with scorn. Work slowed down; productivity dropped.

It was at this time I started appreciating Stephen's managerial qualities. Sharon could not grasp the fact that people different from her could be intelligent and creative irrespective of the obvious differences of age, race, etc., or else she would have placed more emphasis on discovering and developing her team's talents. She would have respected them.

After a year, Sharon relocated to her home country and thus we met Charles. This department operated on a 24-hour, 7-day weekly basis. Someone always had to be on duty. The nature of the job was highly sensitive and we were always under pressure. During Stephen's tenure, we had welcomed the pressure and enthusiastically took on the challenge of mastering it. Sharon had already wounded that spirit. Charles broke it totally. We were now saddled with a manager who could not handle pressure, and so the office was always tense. There was always a lot of shouting going on.

Most of the people we graduate trainees met in that department had been working there for years, and had not received any salary increase or promotion since they started. But people seemed to have only realized this ill usage after Stephen dropped the reins. We had not had any issues with absenteeism with Stephen. People rarely missed a day of work. Now we had stricter rules laid down by Sharon, and Charles' shouting to contend with, yet absenteeism noticeably increased. In the new dispensation, it did not matter if you were ill, you had to be there or have an emergency to explain it. The stricter the rules became, the more people chafed.

After a while, the staff began to complain of being used. They saw Charles as so focused on his own objectives that he did not care about what happened to them. A strange rivalry sprang up between the staff and the manager, and he was isolated. Nobody seemed to care about the company's vision or mission. It was all about reacting to Charles. Anybody found chatting with him was also ostracized and suspected of being a spy. People did less work during work hours. It became common to find people chatting over Google mail or with their Blackberries, or surfing the net. One young lady played several rounds of Solitaire daily.

Even though I had started out in the company excited about being able to relate easily with my manager and loving it, I quickly realized that I now had to stay quite clear of this manager to be accepted. I joined the masses and found much comfort in the solidarity they provided. No one was allowed to work too hard, or he or she would be suspected of trying to please Charles and be ostracized. We all supported anyone he scolded, and in this way, we thrived. By the time the third quarter of the year had reported the same steady decline in productivity as the two preceding ones, Charles came back from a Management Retreat and seemed to have decided to reinvent himself. He began to make an attempt to conciliate people and rally the team. It was too late. We had, in fact, lost our habits of hard work and could not be bothered any longer. A good number of people whom Stephen had identified as high potential contributors to the firm when we first arrived were already interviewing for other jobs and only listened with half an ear to the new Charles. I myself had applied only the previous week for a Masters program in the United Kingdom, which I had initially intended to consider only after getting at least 3 years work experience with the company. I do not think even Stephen could win us back, if he returned to our department now.

## Coffee Quiz

1. What could be the reasons for the differences between Stephen, Sharon, and Charles?
2. How did these differences affect the people who worked with them?

### Dependence, Interdependence, and Complementarity

Conceivably, a man could live on his own, grow his own food, and his own cotton or silk to make his clothes or find some way of otherwise keeping warm, build his own house from scratch, etc. yet most of us would probably agree that this is not the ideal life we would envisage or plan for ourselves. Even when we want to be alone, we still want to have items created by others to supplement or complement what we could produce ourselves—furniture, electricity, housing, food, etc. But beyond these things that are actually external to us as humans, there is also an innate need for others in order to develop to our full potential as human beings. A little baby who lives with wolves (we may have heard of some stories[1] of such) grows up like a wolf, adopting their habits, and perhaps never realizing the possibilities of a human nature. It takes learning from a mother, a father, a family, a school, friends, adversaries, society, etc. to fully develop ourselves, starting with the perception of another (which in turn makes us more conscious of self), or with a language in order to communicate our thoughts and feelings.

We need others. Others need us. Our lives and actions intertwine more and more as technology and development dissolve the boundaries of the world. What is done today in China can affect a stranger on the other side of the world either in the same period of time or in future. This is the sphere of action of the ethical principle—do good and avoid evil. We need to be other-regarding in our actions because it is not sustainable to be otherwise.

We need others. Others need us. Yet we must avoid two dangerous extremes[2]—over-dependence and over-independence. An over-dependent person abdicates self-responsibility and accountability. On the other hand, a person that is too independent runs the risk of losing the valuable contribution that others could make to his life. He may be unable to make friends who could enrich him with their insights into his character, his career path, etc. In the workplace, this is the typical loner. He probably already tends to work better on his own by temperament, and he does not realize when he carries this isolation into all other aspects of work—trusting only his own judgment, refusing to consider other viewpoints, being closed to new ideas unless they come from himself, etc. Very easily, he is lost in his own pride and self-centeredness, no one else matters really. His colleagues are unlikely to like him or to want to be with such a person and thus he is more and more established as a loner. Needless to say, such a person will find it difficult to lead or to manage others. He may not even be able to understand them. This could have a negative impact on his career prospects; there are at times positions in a company to which this kind of person would not be promoted because those in charge are not sure that he would be able to handle the necessary interaction with others that would come with such a move.

Since the mind-set may extend to the home front, the person could also easily lack the support that his family could have provided, having alienated them with his arrogant *"I can help myself; I don't need anybody"* stance, so that, with all the goodwill in the world, they may not notice when he eventually needs help. This could mean a greater likelihood of conflicts at home, which could also impinge on performance at work.

## Teamwork

In a team, the members share a common goal. This is traditionally what is seen to differentiate a team from a group of people who might just have happened to be in the same bus. Many films proceeding from different cultures have been made precisely around this idea of a group of people in a bus, train, or plane who, when they face a common danger or are united by a single objective, become transformed into a team.[3]

### Building Society

An understanding of the social nature of man could help to achieve a reorientation toward seeking what one can do for people rather than what one can get from them. Ethical behavior is predicated on selflessness—an ability to habitually put the common good above our personal interest. It also helps us to understand that people may be helped or even positively transformed by a sense of community at work. An organization in which people feel that others care may enjoy more commitment and altruism than one in which they feel that it is only about fulfilling the strict details of one's contract.

A society built on the premise that each one has to constantly watch his or her back would be a very uncomfortable place to live in. Instead, where there is trust deriving from the knowledge that others will put the common good above their personal good when this is required, it is easier to work together to create viable and mutually beneficial systems and structures.

## Nature and Nurture

Our genetic makeup determines our temperament and therefore to a great extent makes our first reactions (before reason and will intervene) predictable. The environment in which we live and grow also has an impact on us. Researchers and scientists have long studied the interaction of a person's inherited traits with his environment as they affect his behavior.[4] Many of these studies were done with cases of identical twins or adoption. With regard to twins, for example, being brought up in different environments ordinarily leads to their growing up with different habits, tastes, and preferences, having passed through different experiences despite their identical genetic factors. Though they could be similar in nature,[5] (in fact, many identical twins still tend to have different temperaments) the difference in their nurturing would give different hues to their personalities, which would then be completed by the way the choices they may have been making have forged their character.

## Coffee Cues

If each of the different managers could tell their stories, one would be able to see how their temperament and their environment have shaped the kind of manager they have turned out to be. Fortunately, due to the power of freedom, each one can, despite nature and nurture, still make choices, backed by effort and determination, in order to build the character and personality he desires.

## Exercise

Divide into pairs. Within each pair, take turns at telling the other person, in 5 minutes, about the people and events that have made you what you are today.

# CHAPTER 9

# People (Not Assets, Resources, or Capital)

In relating to others, there are many things to take into consideration. The root of all these things is their dignity as human beings. From this flow a number of rights that every human being has.[1] Dignity entails a sense of what is uniquely human, a sense of worth. These rights extend to the people around us who form the society we live in—in the workplace, at home, and in the larger community or the country—and also to the generations to come after us who will share the same human nature that we have and therefore are entitled to our concern. They also have a right to a standard quality of life in an environment conducive to their development.

Since what makes a person human is his rationality, it stands to reason that there is a need to accord equal dignity to people regardless of their financial status, fame, position in the company, or other accidental difference.[2] Differences that are accidental and nonessential (not having regard to rationality that informs the humanity of the person) cannot make a person more or less deserving of human dignity or rights.

Rights in the workplace include rights to privacy, to fair hearing, to procedural justice, to due consideration, etc. At the very minimum, an organization must respect these rights in order to comply with the law. However, organizations that practice humanistic management are likely to think beyond strict observance of the country's laws and to look at what is good for their people. This is of special relevance in instances where some basic and universally agreed human rights are as yet unprotected by law (in theory or in practice or both); for example, where the minimum wage applies only to public companies, where no labor laws address inhumane working conditions or deal with the challenges of child labor, or where there is no legislation preventing an employee from being kept working close to 24 hours (despite his contract having stipulated an 8-hour working day) through the use of new technology such as smart phones.

## Case: Binta

This gives me an opportunity to talk about my Medical Director, who owned the hospital where I worked during my National Youth Service Corps year. Dr. Muri was a tall, dark, cross-eyed man. Nobody liked him; his employees never said one good thing about him. There was this nurse, Binta, whom he liked very much because she did her work diligently and uncomplainingly. She was always on duty, with no day off except weekends. Even on weekends, whenever there was an emergency, she would be among the first people to be called in.

By and by, Binta got married and became pregnant. There was no change to her hectic schedule. I once approached her and asked how she was coping. She said she had complained to Dr. Muri and wished she had more time to rest. Advice came from other staff that she should resign and look for a better job, but apparently there was none in sight at that moment and, according to her, she was just trying to help the Doctor (because they were family friends) and she would manage to cope with the situation. Binta gradually became less efficient; she was at times aggressive with the patients and she got a number of queries regarding this from the Medical Director.

The time came for Binta to give birth. Admitted to our private hospital, she was left in one of the wards. Dr. Muri did not bother to check on her or give her any medication. It was her friend Lami who stayed with her throughout. Binta was in such pain that she could not lie still. The Doctor finally told Lami to take Binta to the Teaching Hospital close by; and all he did was give her transport fare. Binta gave birth 3 hours later to twins. When the news came, we were joyful and could hardly wait for her to come back. Unfortunately, Binta lost her babies. When I saw her again, her face was swollen not only because of sleepless nights but also because of the tears that she could not stop from running down her face. She came to collect her salary (upfront), she said, to bury her children.

To my utmost shock, Dr. Muri refused to pay her; he said that she did not sign any agreement and so it was against the hospital's laws to pay her. As Binta left the hospital, she rained down curses on Dr. Muri and his hospital. She was filled with sorrow and regret. I pitied her very much but was helpless to do anything about the matter.

## Coffee Quiz

1. Was Dr. Muri right to refuse to pay Binta? Please give reasons for your answer.
2. What could the narrator have done? What would you do in his place?

## Dignity and Worth

Dignity means deserving of respect or honor. A person who acts in a dignified way is acting in a way that commands respect. A person who preserves his dignity ensures that he or she does not do anything not deserving of that respect so that he can continue to demand that others respect or honor him. However, when speaking of human dignity, we are referring to the dignity that comes from simply being human, rather than that which is portrayed in the person's actions or words. In other words, while we are concerned with whether someone speaks or acts in a way deserving of respect, we do not lose sight of the fact that his humanity gives him a right to respect on that level. If imprisoned criminals are to be treated with respect (and so they should be), then much more do subordinates deserve respectful treatment despite shortcomings, mistakes, training gaps, etc.

Human dignity is inherently human; it flows from being human—belonging to the human species. A human being is a being of worth, who is the highest being on earth, and thus he always has that dignity of being human and should be treated neither like an inanimate being nor like an animal. Based on the recognition of human dignity, a list of human rights has been postulated through the United Nations Universal Declaration of Human Rights and every country enjoined to respect them. These rights are inalienable and belong to every human being. They include the right to life, the right to free speech, etc.

Organizations need to be respectful of human dignity both in the way they treat their employees and in the way they relate to their customers. Sadly, it is common to encounter some businesses that operate without regard for human dignity because they contradict its very essence. Such would be, for example, a business that thrives on exploitation, such as sweatshops, etc.

### Rights in the Workplace

Because of the dignity the human person has just for being human, we are able to speak of human rights and of duties that we owe others. Apart from the fundamental human rights referred to above, there are many other rights that are not at the same level but are nonetheless rights deriving from our duty to respect others. A few of these rights that relate more to the workplace are explained below. Whenever a right is acknowledged, there is a corresponding duty on the other party to do what it takes to respect that right. The subject of the right also has to respect the same right held by other people.

*Right to privacy:* personal information about employees becomes available to the company during the recruitment process or at other points in time. It is the duty of the company to respect the confidentiality of this relationship and not to allow access to employee records to just anyone. In addition, the company should not pry into the employee's personal life unless there is something that has a direct bearing on his job performance.

*Right to confidentiality with regard to information obtained in the course of employment:* even in the absence of formal agreements, an employee would have a duty to respect confidentiality regarding certain aspects of the business of his employers, for example, trade secrets. Employers often do not leave this to chance, however; they try to incorporate it into formal agreements.

*Right to a fair wage:* sometimes countries stipulate what is a minimum wage. Whether or not this is done, an employer has a duty to pay fair wages. However, opinions differ on what is a fair wage, and as to what should happen if the employer cannot pay what one would consider a fair wage. Would it be better for the person to remain without a job? One possible solution in such cases is that the employer could compensate in other ways for the inability to pay more than he does. For example, he could give accommodation, grant job flexibility, provide career mentoring, health insurance, etc. In some cases, he could give part ownership of the company through the issuance of shares. The employee has a duty to carry out his job conscientiously in order to continue to enjoy the right to fair pay from his employer.

*Right to a fair hearing:* A complaint system—formal or informal—should be put in place so that people can bring up issues that concern them and have them resolved. Fair hearing specifically relates to listening to anyone accused of any misconduct before passing judgment, even mentally.

*Right to a safe and healthy working environment:* companies owe their staff a duty of care—to ensure that the work premises are a safe place to work. For example, they would need to ensure that there is adequate preparation for emergencies such as fire. Psychological safety—freedom from harassment, bullying or verbal abuse, freedom to complain or voice one's thoughts, etc.—is also very important.

*Right to clear job descriptions:* An employee has a right to know clearly what is expected of him, what his job entails. It seems that in some small organizations the management avoids giving employees specific job descriptions so that when unexpected things crop up, they (the staff) will not have this as an excuse to resist additional workload. This is not fair to the people involved.

*Right to be heard and respected for one's opinions:* Even the lowliest staff in the office should not feel undermined or undervalued. Each one contributes his quota to the success of the organization. It was when the sweepers went on strike that the monks of history recognized their indispensability.[3]

*Right to rest:* Staff should not be given so much workload that it is impossible for them to have a life other than in the workplace. This will be discussed further in Chapter 13, where we talk about work.

## Perceptions and Relationships

The human manager must be conscious that co-workers (superiors, colleagues, or subordinates) are not less human than he is. Therefore, he must give everyone a chance to be different, and the space they need to manifest their creativity. In trying to motivate subordinates, he will remain conscious that what works for one may not work for another. He must not only strive to be fair to them but also to be seen as fair. If people perceive a lack of respect or a lack of equity in the way they are treated, they are likely to react by withdrawing and not giving their best to the organization. This is not good for either party.

An employee should also be able to comport himself in a way that commands dignity and respect. It helps him to think positively and have a "can do" spirit. It is to the advantage of organizations that their employees are self-confident and assertive in relating with others. They are better able to represent the company and perhaps even to negotiate on its behalf with other stakeholders such as clients, suppliers, and regulators. Any type of inferiority complex, perhaps produced by such unsavory practices as workplace bullying, is unlikely to help performance.

### Collaboration

Respecting other human beings entails seeing them as other selves and not as tools to achieve what one wants. Hence, human beings should not be manipulated but rather motivated, giving them reasons and helping them see the point of what they are supposed to do. This gives birth to a spirit of collaboration, of partnering within the organization to create value for the customer. People cannot be owned, no matter how many zeros follow the salary figure that the organization pays them.

Clear processes and procedures make it clear to people what they are to expect within the organization and respect their right to be adequately informed about what the organization expects from them. For example, appraisal processes need to be properly constructed so that the people know from the beginning on what criteria they will be assessed. Otherwise, it would be unfair to use those parameters to assess them. Setting targets is another area where the respect for others leads to fairness in setting realistic targets and not setting them up for failure.

### Manners

It is important to behave with decorum, out of respect for others. Manners comprise the rules of social etiquette designed to foster respectful and polite dealings among peoples. They are mostly artificially derived, but are not for this reason without their own relevance.

Among those that are based directly on the need to respect other human beings, we have for example, the demand that it is good manners to arrive punctually at an appointment—such as both for an interviewer and an interviewee, both for the CEO and for the receptionist, etc. or the demand that it is not polite or mannerly to interrupt others while they are speaking. It is bad manners to butt into the conversation of a group. It is bad manners to enter someone else's office without knocking, to borrow someone's property without asking, etc.

Artificial rules include the ways of holding cutlery while dining, etc. These simply satisfy convenience and allow for some standard way of doing things that harmonizes the diversity of all those present in a practical way.

## Coffee Cues

Binta deserved better treatment from the medical director. Dr. Muri was just using her as he would use a machine. He did not respect her as a person with dignity and with rights. He did not consider that she had any claims on him or that he owed her any consideration. She could have been a table in the corner—to be used while useful and to be thrown away once it has outlived its relevance to the organization. Thus, he did not care about her wellbeing even when he could see what she was going through. For example, he could have sent her on maternity leave and found a temporary replacement.

Binta did not insist on being respected either. She did not insist on a maternity leave; she felt she did not have many options. She could not quit the job because she needed the money. However, this does not excuse the behavior of the doctor.

## Exercise

Make a list of the people you interact with on a daily basis. Check the similarities and differences in the way you treat them and try to justify these—for example, if you say good morning to your lecturer but not to your colleagues, reflect on what could be the reason behind this.

# MODULE 3

# Human Progress

# CHAPTER 10

# Setting Personal and Professional Goals

We need to set ambitious human goals for ourselves. This is to say that our goals should be high not merely at the animal level—to eat and drink well, sleep comfortably, etc.—but should be ambitious at the intellectual and moral level. The whole man should progress, in order to attain fulfillment.

The world is filled with a huge variety of goods that could attract us. However, it is clear that they are not all at the same level, as already hinted earlier when explaining about the hierarchy of goods. An ice cream is good (for those who like it) and education is good, but if someone gave up a scholarship to university for a bowl of ice cream, it would sound absurd, if not criminal, to most people. There is an objective hierarchy with regard to the appropriateness of each good to the fulfillment of a human being hinging on how it enriches or undermines human nature, and there is also a subjective hierarchy that would depend on individual tastes and preferences.

We spend most of our lives seeking goods. Errors in our intellectual reasoning or coming from a disordered will or uneducated emotions can affect whether we work towards the goods that are more appropriate for our fulfillment as human beings. Thus a person could work towards goals that are better suited to a dog's nature or to a robot's nature and then realize too late that something is missing from his life. Our limitedness does not allow us to follow two paths at the same time—we must either turn right or left or go zigzag. Since we have only one life, we need to constantly strive to check that we are headed in the right direction to fulfillment.

## Case: Money Needs a Master

Chen had a job at a firm where all that mattered was the bottom line. No one cared about the next person. It was a very superficial environment, and everyone was strongly in competition, sometimes at the expense of the organization. He kept at the job for over 5 years because of the attractive pay, but he never really felt at peace with himself. He had to work long hours, often neglecting the people who were most important to him, his family.

Eventually something happened that made him stop and think.

It was the end-of-quarter and everyone was scurrying to tidy up their balances in order to have an impressive report during the quarterly meeting which the Chief Executive Officer (CEO) always attended. Unfortunately for Chen, his first daughter took ill about a week to the day of the meeting. When it became obvious to Chen that he might not be able to get his report ready, he met with his departmental head, who was completely beside himself with the frenzy of preparing for his own presentation at the meeting. He did not even want to hear of the possibility of Chen missing the deadline.

Chen found this reaction really strange since he had never asked for this kind of concession before, and he was a star employee who had contributed greatly to the excellent performance of the company each year. Also, his daughter was in a life-and-death situation; he could not just go on preparing a report while his daughter lay on her deathbed. He then decided to find a colleague who might be willing to help him put finishing touches to his report in order to avoid a sanction. No one was ready to sacrifice a few hours to help him. Chen was heartbroken. These were the people with whom he had spent the last 5 years of his life, often getting home late and neglecting his family. He applied to take compassionate leave; it was not approved.

He decided to proceed on leave without the requisite approval. After a few days, his daughter died. He sent a letter to his office informing them of the incident and letting them know when he would be able to return to work. One week after his daughter's death, Chen returned to work, only to meet a query on his table. The sight inflamed him; he had finally reached the end of his rope.

He replied to the query but accompanied it with a resignation letter. His departmental head was shocked at his reaction, and called him for a meeting during which he tried to persuade Chen not to walk out on the organization, to no avail. He even offered him a 50% pay raise. But Chen could no longer substitute money for family. He did not even stay the length of his notice, opting instead to pay the organization in lieu. They were very sorry to lose him. They knew they were also losing his customer network.

Chen later took a job with a nongovernmental organization (NGO) close to his family house, and he now takes pride in being able to look at his children's schoolwork and assignments when he returns from the office.[1] His wife is delighted with the transformation of her husband. They are able to spend time with each other, discuss family matters, and make plans together. He also has real friends at his new place of work; the NGO encourages a culture where everyone is his brother's keeper. Chen considers himself a fulfilled man now, even though he has less money at his disposal.

## Coffee Quiz

1. Did Chen make a good choice by resigning in spite of the appeal of his departmental head?
2. Which of the goods involved here could be regarded as being of objective importance, and which would be of subjective importance?

## Aspiring for Fulfillment

We derive fulfillment from striving for and attaining the goods we yearn for. We human beings are beings full of yearnings. We have needs, wants, strivings, for what we think or feel will increase our wellbeing or happiness by fulfilling our longing for physical, psychological, and spiritual goods. For example, a plate of chapatti when one is hungry fulfills a physical need; a hug from a friend when one is grieving fulfills a psychological need, while understanding the market dynamics when one is meeting with a potential business partner fulfills an intellectual and therefore spiritual need. Once we fulfill one longing, another steps into its place and claims our attention, and so on and on so long as there is life in us. We want breakfast, and then we want lunch, or the next breakfast. We want a car, and then we want a house. We want a new pair of glasses, and then we want an extra pair in case the first pair gets broken. We want friends and family to visit and then we want peace and quiet. At times, our desires are even contradictory.

Because we are beings of two dimensions and the spiritual dimension—the intellect and the will—is what sets us apart from other animals and confers on us a special dignity, we can only be truly fulfilled when our immaterial yearnings are satisfied. This is why it is important for us to set ourselves legitimate[2] goals on all three levels—physical, psychological, and spiritual—and not only on one, and to put in the required effort to achieve them, giving special attention and priority to spiritual goals.

One's work plays an important but not exclusive role in one's fulfillment. For this reason, work that makes a person less than human is not appropriate for a human being; it is demeaning. Work that engages a person intellectually as well as physically will tend to bring more opportunities for development and for fulfillment. This can be manifested in different workplace practices and policies and is demonstrated in the organization's concern to ensure fair remuneration for work, ascertain job-person fit, design jobs to include humanly challenging content, etc.

## Failure and Success

What determines failure and success? What is the definition of these words? Some people may consider those who achieve material goods successful while others may consider only those who achieve spiritual goods successful. Having understood the makeup of a human, it is now possible to grasp that real success must have both components in differing proportions; with spiritual fulfillment having the upper hand in determining success if he is to rise beyond the animal plane to be what he truly is capable of being.

## Intrinsic and Instrumental Goods

We want to achieve many things in the world. However, as we said in Chapter 5, goods have a hierarchy. We cannot have everything at the same time. This is primarily because we are limited by our human nature. I may not stay in Chicago relaxing with friends and at the same time watch the

Olympics live in London even if the two are good. Some goods are good in themselves, intrinsically good, while some are good as instruments to obtain the intrinsic goods. The intrinsic goods can be listed as follows: life, knowledge, play, aesthetic experience, harmony with other people, intelligent control of one's life, and harmony with a transcendent being.[3] Choices of extrinsic goods should be such that they enable one to acquire intrinsic goods. Any choice that focuses exclusively on extrinsic goods may need to be reassessed to discover if it is worthwhile. Needless to say, if an instrumental good compromises one's ability to attain an intrinsic good, it is probably not worthwhile. In general, instrumental goods are very useful; they solve a good number of problems and provide us some measure of happiness.

Because human nature is not totally material, it cannot be fulfilled by goods that are totally material. This explains the unsatisfying experience that accompanies material possessions—in the sense that once we possess them, we want something else. While the person wants a pair of shoes, he feels that he would be happy once he possesses them, but once they are in his cupboard or he has worn them once, he realizes that his desires are already redirected towards some other targeted acquisition. The intrinsic goods are a better complement to us in this regard and therefore the satisfaction derived from them lasts much longer.

Extrinsic goods or instrumental goods also are characterized by a scarcity component—they naturally inspire competitiveness since they can only be possessed by one person at a time. If I get the shoes, then you do not get them. The same applies to a certain status, prestige, promotion, money, etc. However, for intrinsic goods, usually there is an abundance component that allows many different people to have access to them simultaneously and in an unlimited way. Thus, for example, the enjoyment of music is open to as many people as imaginable, and the same applies to growth in knowledge, rewarding work, healthy religious experiences and friendships, etc.

The sources of extrinsic fulfillment are very often outside the person and make the person dependent on others for these goods. For example, one's prestige is predicated on one's acknowledgment by society. Several people could make the same contribution to humanity and perhaps only one would be accorded that prestige and the others ignored. Someone may deserve to be promoted and end up being overlooked. This is a fragile basis on which to depend for something as critical to a human being as fulfillment. The sources of intrinsic fulfillment, being more internal and more within the control of the person, may for this reason be more lasting in their effects and therefore in their relevance to human happiness.

Thus, a manager who understands the concept of fulfillment as it affects human beings will not focus solely on extrinsic rewards in the attempt to motivate people.

## Coffee Cues

Chen's employers did not take into account that what fulfills a human being must include intrinsic good and not only instrumental good. The company thought that success meant wealth, and they were shocked that Chen could leave them to go elsewhere. Due to their insensitivity, they lost a very good hand. They may even have seen him as a failure when he left their firm to work for an NGO, for a lower salary. Chen himself, and his family, were happier. The firm assumed that they could treat their employees however they liked as long as they paid the right amount of money. They were wrong in their assumption. They could have avoided losing Chen simply by treating him as a human being and therefore acknowledging his need to have a family and care for them.

Like Chen, we all aspire for fulfillment. However, like him also, at times we settle for less without realizing it and we are reluctant to take the steps that will lead to a change. Chen initially thought he could find fulfillment by amassing wealth (extrinsic goods), but he later discovered that relationships with family and friends (intrinsic goods) were more important to him. Instrumental goods should not be placed as ends in themselves; they need to be subservient to the intrinsic goods.

We see from this case again that man is a social being. Chen realized, at first only vaguely, that he wanted more than just money; he wanted a relationship with his colleagues. And so, he was not fulfilled at his workplace. Yet, he could not blame anyone for what happened to him. It was his choice to stay with the company, just like it was his choice to leave when he eventually opened his eyes to what was really good for him. He chose his family and walked out on a system that saw him as a mere economic tool, one more machine.

## Exercise

Make a list of the goods in which you are interested, and classify them as either intrinsic or extrinsic goods. Now, assign weights to the importance of each of these goods for attaining your most important goals, and then examine what means you could use or are using to achieve these goals, how suitable the means are, and how much effort you put in them.

# CHAPTER 11

# Choosing the Means

As discussed in Chapter 5, man usually acts with purpose. He is the only animal free to achieve his goals. For any one goal, he usually has a variety of means that he could use. If the means he chooses are not optimal, they affect the achievement of his goal. If they are inappropriate for what is humanly good, then they taint his goal with a negative moral qualification even if he attains it. The end does not justify the means. Using the wrong means also leaves a mark on the person—he finds it easier to adopt the wrong means in future and more difficult to act right.

## Case: Team Chad—Free Agents

Helmut was reading the report he had requested—an explanation of why Team Chad's performance had been dropping in the past months. He did not expect what he found in it. According to the report, the performance drop was due to a change in the supervisor of Team Chad.

Team Chad was one of the teams of online customer service representatives at Maddox Telecoms Ltd. Their job entailed educating customers about products and resolving their queries over the phone. The performance of a call representative was judged by the quality of service he or she gave to a customer. This was rated on a scale of 1 to 100 and results were sent to the person concerned at the end of every month by the quality assurance team who evaluated random calls chosen during the month. Representatives were distributed into teams of 20 each and each team was assigned a supervisor. A team's performance was rated by taking the average of every member's quality rating; and a team score of 100 was rewarded with a bonus at the end of the month.

After spending some minutes revising again how the teams worked and were rated, Helmut reread the sheets in front of him:

"When Hans was assigned as team supervisor, he gathered the team for a meeting where we collectively deliberated on which rules would govern the team. Each member made suggestions. At the end, we had a set of rules, and we decided on the fines to be paid when a rule was broken. Hans also warned us about the importance of the team quality score and let us know that he wanted the team always to score 100. He emphasized that we should look at the big picture and never be satisfied with getting 100 on individual quality scores; only 100 as a team would impress him. Going on, he suggested that each week, a different member of the team should give a presentation on one of the company's products. The team agreed and we made a schedule for this activity. He also encouraged us to sit together and wake each other up after breaks when working through the night.

"The performance of the team, on Hans's watch, was superb. Each member was well informed about company products and services. The team always scored high in the quality ratings. Whenever the team failed to score 100, the person in the team who did not make the 100 score would quickly send an apology to everybody without being prompted. There was a strong bond among everyone. Anybody who broke a team rule would pay the prestipulated fines they had agreed on without the slightest protest. Everyone was friends with everyone. Unlike other teams, Team Chad did not have a team representative because we could not decide who to single out as the one who had the interests of the team most at heart.

"Whenever anybody in the team encountered a problem, held a celebration, or engaged in any activity that required financial support, the money accumulated from fines collected from team rule offences was added to whatever donation the team decided to give to the person. It was a rule to meet at the person's house to rejoice or mourn with the person. For example, the whole team attended my daughter's first-year birthday party, and they took a photograph with her. Performance as a team was outstanding and after the first few months of Hans, Team Chad was getting emails from the quality assurance team commending us for a job well done. I remember always feeling happy on my way to work.

"In January last year, there was a reshuffle in teams. We were assigned a new supervisor and a few members of our team were replaced with members of another team. Our new supervisor was a lady named Surangi. We heard that she was strict and was someone who enforced the company policies to the letter. In our first meeting together, she confirmed the rumors. She told us that everything we might have heard about her was probably true but that if we followed her rules, we would have no problem. She read out our contract agreement to us at the meeting and gave us a set of rules to follow. She told us that any defaulter would be issued a query and that after a certain limit, he or she would be 'kicked out.' She asked each member of the team to summarize the minutes of the meeting and send it to her email box. She then distributed drinks to every member of the team. We later received an email with an attachment, informing us that we were now scheduled to have individual coaching sessions with her, where she would assess and train us on our knowledge of company products.

"This is when Team Chad's performance began to falter. At first many team members still got individual scores of 100, but this did not last. The team as a whole never scored 100 even though there was a reward offered by the supervisor for getting a 100 score. People began to find excuses not to work within Surangi's range, for fear of making a mistake and getting a query. In one instance, a lady named Paloma was queried for having nylon bags on her office table. The nylon bags contained clothes she brought to the office to sell to her colleagues after working hours. She ignored the query and quarreled bitterly with the supervisor when confronted. She eventually resigned saying that she could not work with Surangi. Rashid, another member of the team, was sacked after a customer complained that he was given wrong information. When I asked him about it, Rashid said that he could not attend to the customer properly because he did not like the way Surangi spoke to him earlier that day and that this affected him. Team members at times still attended one another's functions; the supervisor was never invited to these events."

## Coffee Quiz

1. What is micromanagement?
2. Does anything in the case study remind you of the "carrot and stick" approach to managing people?

## Beyond Temperament and Environment

We already saw in earlier chapters that despite the fact that each person's character and personality are molded by genetics (including inherited traits from parents, grandparents, etc.) and his environment (parents, extended family, schools, social groups, and society), these are not explanatory enough of human actions. There is another element that comes into play—one's free choices. Free choice is enabled by the possession of the intellect and the will. One is able to know and then to direct one's will to the pursuit of what one knows to be good because it is directed towards one's fulfillment.

Each choice we make takes us closer to or further away from our ultimate purpose of fulfillment, as happens with a person at a crossroads. A step in the right direction facilitates progress in the right direction and reduces the likelihood of losing the way. A step in the wrong direction, on the other hand, facilitates further steps in the wrong direction and therefore takes the person further away from his destination. The person can change direction but it is twice as arduous to get back to the right track—effort to retrace steps and the effort to take steps in the right direction despite the weariness brought on by the steps already taken in the opposite direction. The recognition that our choices shape our lives helps us to see why we should strive to consistently make choices that are in consonance with the kind of person we want to be, and why we should make the effort to retrace our steps if and when we deviate.

Since no matter which direction one takes it is the good that one perceives that motivates one to make the effort the movement entails, it is of vital importance to educate the intellect and the will rightly in order to be able to use freedom wisely, to be able to make ethically responsible and sustainable decisions personally, professionally, and for the organization.

## Freedom

Freedom is the ability to determine ourselves, to decide the direction in which we will take our steps. There are people who are afraid to choose, hesitating to take decisions, perhaps because they dread the responsibility that comes with free choice and so they prefer to remain standing at the crossroads. However, whenever one is tempted not to choose or to unreasonably delay choosing, it is important to realize that, apart from the lack of productivity of such a course of action, sitting on the fence is itself a choice that brings its own consequences. For example, when we do nothing to safeguard our environment, we cannot be surprised later if we make our world uninhabitable now or for the future.

Being aware of every human being's freedom helps us to be alert to the duty to respect others' choices. For example, an employee may wish to change jobs. It is a choice he is making and has a right to make. At the same time, one may at times have some knowledge than he has not and this could lead one to try to persuade him that it is better to choose to stay where he is—usually by giving him more information so that he can see the superior good that is proffered. As has been hinted above in Chapter 4 on knowledge and truth, the ability to make right choices depends on one's ability to seek sound knowledge in order to strengthen one's intelligence. Yet in the end the person should be left free to decide—that is part of respecting the person's human dignity. This respect for other's free choices should extend to customers and other stakeholders too.

There is a clear delineation between manipulation, such as trying to change an individual's inclinations and preferences without reckoning with his or her power of free choice, and legitimate persuasion, which respects the person's freedom. In the drive to achieve managerial or organizational objectives, managers must not lose sight of the need to acknowledge and respect everyone's power of choice.

### License and Responsibility

Each person, in exercising the freedom to choose what he wants, must at the same time be aware that every choice carries with it some measure of responsibility. When a person wishes to choose without being responsible for those choices, what the person wants is a license. The responsibility for the actions would then be shifted to the giver of the license. But freedom is not license. If one jumps off a roof, one is responsible for the broken knee that follows. Companies that produce pollutants are responsible for all the contamination caused by the pollutants and for the ecosystems destroyed by the contamination, and for the livelihoods affected by the destruction of those ecosystems, even if the physical distances between the company and the end-users are very large and even if the company had no direct intention to harm those people.

Looking at another example, a job seeker who has educated his emotions and understood freedom may not jump at an offer just because of the immediate or short-term satisfaction that he will get out of having found a job or being able to earn money, but may rather intelligently assess whether the offer is worth accepting, evaluating the consequences that will accompany it and being ready to accept the responsibilities.

Responsibility is a consequence of freedom; we expect a certain level of rational behavior because we know that human beings have a choice. This is why there are sanctions for irrational behavior and prisons. We do not need prisons for beings who cannot choose, who merely follow the laws of their nature, as chickens and horses do. They always do the right thing for themselves. We do not charge them with the burden of responsibility. If a hyena were to bite off a puma's ear, or even to attack a man, it would make no sense to require him to defend himself in court, or to ask forgiveness for the offence. Ought implies can. Without can, there can be no ought.

### Constraints

A constraint is a limit to freedom. We human beings are limited—we cannot do everything we might have liked to do—for example, we cannot grow wings and fly. The freedom of a limited being is to be understood within the constraints that limit the being. Some of these limits are physical, others are social, and yet others are political. Among the social are contractual constraints.

Physical constraints include the laws of the basic sciences, such as the laws of biology and the laws of physics. A man is free, but he cannot choose not to digest his food when he eats it; neither can he choose not to fall when he jumps off the roof. Scientific innovations tend to attempt to overcome these limits—hot air balloons, planes, and parachutes. In doing so, they count on other laws inherent in the material order, for example, what force it takes to overcome the force of gravity, etc.

Social limits come from the social order—the relationship of a person with those around him, with his domestic surrounds (his family and his organization) and with his polis (law and order in the city), for example, the neighbor's compound, the city's traffic laws.

When freedom is exercised, it triggers new constraints. When a person enters a car to travel from London to Nottingham, he is constrained from at the same time traveling on a train from London to Manchester or strolling in Kew Gardens. The choice of one seat in the first coach limits the possibility of being seated in another in the second coach, etc.

## Commitment

The exercise of freedom always carries within it an element of commitment. This is aptly illustrated by a simple analogy. An MBA graduate attends a job interview and receives an offer letter from the company. He accepts their offer and signs the contract of employment. In choosing to sign, he has freely committed himself to the content of the contract, and mutual obligations are thus created between him and the company. The same would apply to anyone who signed a contract unless he did not have the ability to contract due to age or some impairment of reasoning capacity, or if he was forced, that is, either his knowledge or his will was not fully engaged in the process. Freedom is effective when one fulfils what is committed to in spite of possible difficulties.

A mature person strives to fulfill his commitments. A person who enters into commitments and never fulfills them would at the very least be regarded as a foolish person by those who observe him. It would be difficult for him to find people to take him seriously and enter into business dealings with him unless he always approaches new people each time, people who do not know him. The best marketing a company can get is the referrals from satisfied customers who can testify that the company fulfills its commitment to deliver value to its customers.

## Active and Passive Freedom

We could describe freedom from two perspectives—the active and passive. Active freedom would mean freedom for action, for actualizing one's potential. It would usually require commitment and considerable and persevering effort to earn this freedom. Without such effort, one's freedom would be limited. Thus, for example, one could actively study in order to actualize one's possibility of becoming a doctor. Without studying, the freedom to become a doctor is given up and one's sphere of freedom is narrower because it then excludes all the possible futures that depend on studying. Conversely, the choice to study opens the person up to a bigger space for the exercise of freedom because it confers on him a wider range of options for a future career. Likewise, sports people exercise and follow diets in order to keep as fit as they need to be to perform at their best. They are giving up something, and perhaps even engage in activities they may find disagreeable, but they are ready to go through this because of the worthy and fulfilling goals they have set themselves. Active freedom is at times referred to as "freedom for" because the person embraces constraints in order to be free for the development and achievement of his inherent potential, to be free to excel.

On the other hand, passive freedom is more externally driven and results from escaping constraints. It is a freedom from external encumbrances, from suffering, pain, poverty, etc.; its focus is survival and wellbeing. Thus, passive freedom tends to take care of physical and psychological needs. It is important and often is a preliminary goal in life especially when one has been deprived of it. However, when a person views anything that requires sacrifice and pain as confining and to be avoided, the person's space for freedom is narrowed until he lives mostly at the animal level. The fact is that many worthwhile objectives in life can only be attained by dint of hard work, self-discipline, and a determined struggle. Thus, for example, the path of early maturity often includes the realization as one passes from childhood to adolescence that the drive to achieve one's life goals has to come from within and not from a fear of punishment by mommy or daddy.

The two perspectives are not mutually exclusive and while it is true that a hungry man may find it difficult to apply himself to seeking wisdom, he would increase his chances of fulfillment more if he could find within himself the determination to do so in spite of his difficult circumstances than if he did not. If Ben Carson had waited to be free from poverty before applying himself to his books (encouraged by his mother), he might have lost his freedom to be a doctor long before they established themselves at a comfortable level in life.[1]

At the same time, one could achieve passive freedom and still be unfulfilled because of having failed to activate the earned freedom that helps to actualize oneself, the one that develops the person in a richer or more lasting way and pertains more to the rational side of man. Even when David[2] was no longer in the concentration camp and was living with a rich family and enjoying wealth and security for the first time in his life, it is clear that while he is no longer restricted, hungry, exhausted, etc., he still lacked fulfillment because he needed to know and be known, and to love and be loved, in order to really grow as a person.

### Inhibitors of Freedom

Freedom can be inhibited by whatever incapacitates the intellect or the will, such as ignorance, manipulation, or coercion. The more the intellect or the will is hampered, the less free the person is. Incapacitation may be so heavy that the person is no longer free (at least externally where force is concerned) and is therefore not responsible for his actions,[3] for example, actions carried out at gunpoint—the passion of fear has over-ridden the person's knowing and willing. Yet even in the case of extreme force, there always remains a little space within which the person remains free to reject what he is being forced to do. This is interior freedom— a true freedom that cannot be taken away from a person. This is what Viktor Frankl experienced and wrote about in the account of his stay in a concentration camp.[4]

## Choices and Values

Above, we have seen that human beings have the power to choose in every circumstance, even when it does not seem obvious. Not making a choice is a choice in itself. A repetition of choices makes it easier to incline to that choice, as it were leaving deep grooves in the person's substance, so that a series of wrong choices flaws the person's future choosing capacity.

It is important to consider the effects of one's choices in the long run and not just look at immediate effect or benefits. Sustainability and responsibility require this ability.

For a person who wishes to live a life of consideration for others, choices should not be based on personal objectives alone but rather on true relations of mutuality in which the true interests of all the parties are taken into consideration and nobody is treated as a pure instrument for the interest of others. Otherwise, the wishes would remain mere rhetoric, as happens at times with corporate statements of core values.

## Locus of Control and Action

We already mentioned locus of control in Chapter 5 and made reference to the advisability of developing a locus of control that is more internal than external. Understanding freedom and how to use it effectively is related to this. Moreover, if one has a tendency to an external locus of control, recognizing this is the beginning of counteracting it. Having greater self-awareness, one can consciously and deliberately make choices both personally and career-wise. The first step is perhaps to discover the things that are most important to you, and then make choices that allow these important aspects of your life to flourish. Since each human being ultimately has only one life and personal life cannot be completely separated from career or work life, one will be careful in these choices.

For example, one might decide to seek work in environments where one would not have to sacrifice the good of the family for the good of the organization or one might be looking for an environment that allows one to grow and thrive. One might decide to pay less attention to extrinsic goods. This requires actually beginning to pay more attention to the intrinsic, and doing this repeatedly so that it becomes a habit.

In essence, one takes control of one's life by having a largely internal locus of control.

## Coffee Cues

The members of Team Chad initially would freely carry out the tasks they had committed to and would freely apologize when they failed to live up to their commitments. An atmosphere of mutual respect and of responsible behavior was fostered by allowing the exercise of freedom.

## Project

Read *Man's Search for Meaning*, by Viktor Frankl, and comment on his experience.

# CHAPTER 12

# Scripting and Re-Scripting Self

The choices one makes tend to coalesce into habits when they are repeated. Thus, one who repeatedly makes choices that disregard others becomes habitually selfish, while one who keeps making choices that are selfless will develop those habits. Bad habits are traditionally referred to as vices while good habits are called virtues. Choices operationalized in habits (of virtue or vice) show the real person. No matter what values the person verbally professes, we can tell what his real values are from the choices he makes. It is in this sense that we script our selves and determine what we are.

It is always possible, however, to change the direction of one's choices and re-script one's self, though it may be more or less difficult depending on how strong a habit has been formed. Just as it is normally easier and faster to destroy than to build (the twin towers for example) it is easier to acquire habits that go against true human fulfillment than those that work for it. It could be easier to lie in bed when one ought not than to jump up, shower, and get ready to face the traffic going to work. Yet, being rational, one is able to look beyond the attractiveness of staying in bed and make the choice of going through the stress of getting up and going to work.

The same action would be more difficult for a person who has been lazing in bed for months than for one who has been habitually getting up early to reach the office on time. Yet it is never too late for the slugabed to begin to train himself to get up by putting in the effort it requires until it becomes somewhat easier and even perhaps becomes his default mode. In order to do this, he may need to be better informed[1] of the future good consequences of his effort or helped to achieve the target once or twice so that he can experience the feeling of having succeeded and be motivated to keep on trying even in the face of occasional failure.

There are some habits that one needs to acquire in order to develop character. Four of them we could call master habits, since they enable the possessor to acquire self-mastery and to lead self and others right. In fact, we are constantly growing in character. Not noticing or caring which habits we develop can make life very difficult for us—especially when we do not understand why certain things happen. For example, someone could say, *"I don't know why this woman hates me; she always finds fault with whatever I say; she does not understand me,"* and perhaps the problem is that the speaker lacks patience and always loses her temper while explaining things, before the other person can grasp what has been said.

## Case: It's a Tough World

Halima worked as a marketer in a new generation bank in Nigeria. She was a married woman of high morals who frowned at anything she perceived as contrary to her religious values. She did not actually read her Quran every day, but she ensured she practiced its tenets as much as she could. She had lately started following the public debate about Islamic banking and was considering, albeit not very seriously, whether she ought not to continue working with her current employers. She worked hard and was mostly happy with her growth so far in the organization in the 3 years she had been employed there. Only a few issues bothered her.

One of her greatest challenges was that, as a marketer, she was often under great pressure to meet her given targets. Her team leader was harsh and indulged habitually in verbally abusing his direct reports. He never minced words in telling her just how stupid he thought her, seeming to believe that by demeaning her he was challenging her to do anything to bring in new accounts. Halima generally ignored him at times like this. Several times, he tried to set her up with lascivious men, who clearly wanted her to trade her body for their accounts. She always refused, and the boss criticized her for being unrealistic. She tried to spend as little time as possible worrying about these instances, since jobs were hard to get and she did not want to be a career mom. So far, she was meeting her targets anyway, though sometimes by the skin of her teeth. After a while, he desisted, and she was more at peace at her job. He even seemed to have changed his values, since he now praised her occasionally and had been heard by a colleague publicly deriding people who got customers' accounts through unethical means.

One day a few months later, an apparently very wealthy potential customer visited the bank and then left after speaking with her team leader for a few minutes. About 10 minutes later, she was summoned by her team leader and asked to meet the customer at his hotel to obtain the details for his account over lunch. Thinking that it was sure to be a business lunch, Halima left for the hotel. She had lunch with the customer but he appeared reluctant to talk about the account while the food was being served or while they were eating. Halima stopped probing and resigned herself to be patient. Even if they discussed business after the lunch ended, she would still get back to the office long before closing time. After the meal he suggested that they retire to his room. Shocked, Halima inquired why. He looked quizzically at her and told her that, if she wanted his account, she had to sleep with him. All her entreaties fell on deaf ears, and she stormed out of the hotel.

On getting back to the bank, Halima reported the incident in righteous anger to her team leader, expecting him to commend her for her decision to be faithful to her husband. On her way to his office, a sympathetic colleague commented that she should switch on her phone recorder. She thought she would not need it since her boss had changed his ways, but she did it anyway. She had a huge disappointment when he flared up and asked her to either sleep with the customer and get his account, or hand in her resignation letter by the next morning. Thankfully, her phone recorder worked throughout the duration of the conversation.

Scared but spirit unbroken, Halima took a risk and reported her boss to her branch manager. The following morning, he was summoned and by the end of the day, he had been recommended for immediate retrenchment. Since she was no longer sure that nothing would threaten her values at this bank, Halima decided to resign. She did so 3 months later. Luckily, in spite of the ever-rising unemployment rates in the country, she got a job shortly afterwards. It paid much less than the bank; but she no longer experienced the tension of working in a place where her principles clashed with those of many people around her. The new job also allowed her to spend more time with her family.

## Coffee Quiz

1. What do you think helped Halima in the decisions she took?
2. What virtues are required to blow the whistle when in a situation that calls for it?

# Managing Prudently

Prudence is the master habit that regulates others by helping the person to discern what the right thing to do in each situation is. Training in decision making often calls for the development of habits of prudence—looking at things from the different possible angles; considering the soft issues as well as hard numbers; looking at the short-term and long-term implications of decisions to be taken now and their sustainability economically, socially, and environmentally; foreseeing the consequences and the possible effects on all the people involved or affected; considering the common good of the society of which the business is striving to be a responsible citizen.

### Implementing Core Values

Organizations frequently espouse some values that they declare to be the core values of the company. Discerning which values should be adopted as a company's core values is an important stage of the setting up of the company. After selecting the values, the organization then has the challenge of ensuring that they are implemented throughout the company. The management team will have to select the best way to do this. These decisions all require prudence.

### Taking Difficult Decisions

After a prudent decision has been taken, it might still be difficult to implement it. For example, a manager may decide that it is more prudent to tell his boss that the budget they agreed to at the beginning of the year is unrealistic now because of certain changes in the market dynamics, rather than to wait until sales actually fall drastically. Yet, it may be a difficult thing for him to undertake, if his boss is not a patient kind of person. Or a supervisor may deem it more prudent to tell a star staff that the promotion he had hoped for has for good reasons been bestowed on his colleague, rather than to wait for him to hear of it from the grapevine; yet he may find it very difficult to face up to this task. The master habit one needs to develop in order to take and implement difficult decisions is known as fortitude. It is constituted by strength of character.

One requires strength and the self-discipline that comes with it in many different situations—to face irate shareholders calmly; to argue rationally in board meetings or management team meetings; to communicate with customers who are irritating without losing one's temper; to apologize to very upset customers when the company is at fault; to face angry union officials; to announce bad news to staff, for example, about not paying out a bonus at the end of the year; to remain patient with difficult employees and inconsistent bosses; to work on or read a boring report; to respond pleasantly to unpleasant colleagues; to smile at others at work when experiencing a headache; etc.

### Golden Mean

One of the challenges of managing people is to find the just balance between extremes. A manager requires a willingness to be fair in order to give everyone around him what is due to them, for example, to discern and act justly as to when to insist on processes and procedures being strictly followed and when to let go despite the risk of setting a precedent and still maintain fairness and equity. After all, it is impossible to treat every person and every situation always the same. This master habit is called justice. It is not always feasible to be perfectly just, since human beings are not perfect and do not have perfect knowledge of every situation, but if one is at least seen to be trying, it will go a long way to assure and reassure people that they will be fairly treated.

## Maturity and the Best Self

Each person is constantly developing and growing as time passes. When the person's character is tempered as he grows older, we say that the person is becoming mature. Since each person possesses different temperaments and inclinations that do not disappear with the passage of time, though as discussed in earlier chapters they can be brought under control and they can be educated, the challenge facing each individual is actually that of becoming the best self they can be. This often requires being measured and controlled in one's reactions, being temperate. If a manager goes around saying *"I'm hot-tempered and that's it,"* and does not put in the effort required to moderate his resulting aggression, he may easily find that after a certain point in his career, the organization sets him aside and is unwilling to promote him to higher positions of greater responsibilities. This is likely to be because of the magnitude of the company's exposure to the risks of him losing his temper at the wrong time when he is in more sensitive positions. Temperance is a master habit because it is the habit that enables a man to be king of himself and of his own inclinations and to moderate his tendencies and retain the control of himself that is essential if he is not to be enslaved by any of his passions and appetites.

## Applying Knowledge

We know through what our senses tell us from their connection with our environment. Applying this knowledge requires us to make judgments. Making judgments requires the skills discussed earlier—wisdom or prudence,[2] justice, fortitude, and temperance. A CEO who gets carried away by excessive attachment to his own opinion or to personal tastes may easily make some decisions that are not optimal for the organization. Knowing himself well enough to realize whether or not he has such tendencies and then exercising the will power to curtail them when they threaten to manifest will help him increase his self-knowledge and self-control and therefore help him achieve responsible management.

### Consistency

An interest in being fair makes one appreciate the value of consistency. Many perceptions of injustice in organizations come precisely from observing inconsistencies in those who represent the organization. For example, staff may see that the management has interpreted and applied different principles to the same situation because it happened at different times or because it involved different people. Such arbitrariness leads to perceived unfairness and a drop in trust levels.

## Virtuous Management

Organizations are made up of people, and the decisions that determine what the organization does are taken by the people at the helm of affairs in that organization. The more virtuous these people are, the greater the likelihood that the organization will act ethically, responsibly, and sustainably in society. In short, the practice of habits of good management by the managers in an organization results in virtuous management and contributes toward establishing the kind of culture that makes for a virtuous organization.

## Developing People

In an organization where these habits are prized, it is very probable that one will also find an interest in helping those who work there to develop these habits. The interest may be simply in order that they may take optimal decisions that benefit the company. However, whatever the reason behind it, training people to develop good managerial habits will benefit the people themselves beyond the office needs. This is because the skills thus practiced and learned are transferable skills that the person can apply in other facets of his life—at home, in social groups, etc.—and in each case, they will help to make him successful in whatever he tries to achieve and cause others to admire and respond positively to him.

Other good habits that help human beings to progress toward their fulfillment include humility, diligence, sincerity, patience, order, etc. The good news is that good habits are developed somewhat in solidarity—what this means is that developing one makes it easier to develop others. At times, one has to be careful to ascertain which areas one needs to develop in; for example, someone could think that he is very humble and overlook the possibility that the reason he does not give his opinion in management meetings is because he is afraid of making a mistake and looking foolish (which actually reflects pride), or someone may congratulate himself in being able to control his wine intake at official functions and not realize that he is incapable of restraint when olives are served (his gluttony is simply manifested in ways different from those of a habitual tippler). In a similar way, a boss who believes that he is a good and benevolent superior to his subordinates may be surprised to realize that he is good and benevolent only so long as they think exactly like him,[3] in which case he is actually a selfish person who does not respect others' freedom and cannot bear a new staff who, not realizing the kind of person he is, starts by speaking up frankly and disagreeing with the boss.

## Coffee Cues

We cannot expect to drop negative habits or pick up positive ones overnight. Time and effort is indispensable for the achievement of either of these two goals. Knowing oneself is important in order to be alert to the choices we repeat and the habits we may be unconsciously forming, and also in order to consciously form the habits that we may need in order to be better persons, better managers, and better citizens of our country and of our world.

## Exercise

List 10 good habits you know of that could help a manager to manage people or resources optimally. Reflect on each one of the ten in order to identify which one(s) of the four master habits—prudence, justice, fortitude, and temperance—it could have a link to. Give examples of situations or events in which each of these ten habits would come in handy.

Example:

| Habit | Master habit | Reflection | Situation |
|---|---|---|---|
| Keeping working papers tidy, in the right place. | Fortitude | It requires strength: the discipline to do it even when tired after a hard day, or when upset with colleagues, or when feeling lazy. | One might be required to produce information at short notice. |

# CHAPTER 13

# The Manager at Work

People spend most of their day at work. Hence, this is a very important setting for their development as human beings. If a person does not improve himself at work and through his work, then either the person remains the same, which is a bit unlikely and in any case unworthy of a human being, or the person becomes worse. As people develop themselves and become better, they also act more responsibly and as better citizens they build a better society. If they become worse, the society is thereby impoverished.

This chapter discusses aspects of people management that have to do with the conduciveness of a workplace to the integral development of the staff. Among the many possible aspects, we have selected job-person fit, rewarding work, value congruence, and workplace culture for inclusion here. As usual, we will begin by reflecting on a case study narrating a concrete workplace experience. We also later on consider briefly work that produces what is harmful to humanity.

## Case 1: The "One-man Business"

Often I have heard people complain about one issue or the other regarding "one-man businesses," and after working in one I started to see their reasons. The complaints varied; some complained about salaries not being paid on time, some complained about having to work extra hours outside office time. For me, my major problem was with the structure, organization, and planning within the organization (most of the time, there was none). I believed that if these things were to be set in place then the operations of the company would be smoother. This is not to say that all one-man businesses face these challenges—I just happened to be in one that did.

I worked with an IT company that specialized in developing software applications and systems integrations. However, while I was working there, the major product the company was developing and marketing was call/contact center solutions. We usually had to work overtime, closing long after 5 o'clock, almost on a regular basis. However, when a colleague had to attend to something very urgent within working hours, which happened seldom, I noticed that these requests were not usually granted and often the management, in this case our boss, would say: *"You either want to work or you don't; and, if you don't, quit."* He was forgetting that on a daily basis he was cutting into your own free time when you would have attended to these personal needs and not have had to wait until they became so urgent and pressing that they now required your attention during working hours.

As much as I was not of the opinion that people should do other things during office hours, I also thought it was not fair that he did not grant some of these requests, and what happened eventually was that one by one some of the staff began to leave. Our employer was thinking basically about himself and the organization forgetting that we, the staff, had other areas of life we needed to live outside the office. As we have learned in the Nature of Human Beings, we should always consider others when making decisions and we should not use our power of freedom to oppress people.

I see this issue as a problem of structure and planning, because, if there was a time frame created for office hours, then the organization should try and restrict itself to this timing. And only on days where a very important project is coming up should you mandate people to stay long after their closing hours. And let it be that if anyone wants to stay beyond the working hours to complete a certain task they do so voluntarily. This would help them exercise their freedom to choose, even though it is within certain constraints. They would tend to perform better.

However, the extra time and effort put in by us, the staff, was not entirely a loss. During all this, more knowledge was gained, the threshold for handling pressure increased, making us tougher individuals capable of handling certain challenging circumstances, hence, building a stronger personality. All the knowledge gained will go with us wherever we go, even after leaving the job in question, and no one can take that away from us.

But the major problem was that the job description for each individual was not spelled out and, as orders came from above, they had to be followed.

However, the sequence or number of the orders at each particular time was unknown, as no one knew the mind of our employer, and I believe that this is what affected the whole structure of the organization. The main reason for this was that our employer felt that he was the only one who understood what his dreams were, and so only he knew what had to be done and how it should be done. He hired a manager who was to take charge of some situations/challenges in the office, but he hindered him from doing his work by also trying to do the same job. I remember that there was a time he had to travel out of the country for a business organization for about 1 week. Even while he was there he tried to "direct" the affairs of things in the office. He wanted to conduct every affair, not leaving room for each individual to bring out their creativity, hence getting less from people rather than more. And when he finally came back, he regarded everything that had been done in his absence as a waste of time, refusing to acknowledge the amount of work each individual had put into the task.

Having recognized that the major problem was in the structuring of the organization, and that each person's job had to be defined in order for productivity to increase and for pressure to be reduced within the system, the manager he had hired tried to tell him about the changes that needed to be made. But he (the manager) was rebuffed by the MD, who said he knew how to run his organization and that he did not need anyone to tell him how to go about that. He refused to admit that knowledge can be gained from anyone, even from the mouth of a child. He also allowed his vice—of pride—to prevent him from learning what would make both himself and his organization better.

## Coffee Quiz

1. Why do you think that the MD resisted taking the suggestions of the manager?
2. How important are structure and planning in an organization?

## Psychological Success

At times, one hears of apparently very successful career people who experience crises late in life when they realize that they have achieved the wrong goals or have focused on one goal to the detriment of another that is equally important to their fulfillment.[1]

### Job-Person Fit

When a person seems to be unhappy or unproductive at work, it is possible that the problem is that the person has been placed in a wrong role. Before resorting to solutions like laying off the person, an organization that understands human nature will want to see if this is the case. For example, a person employed for the Accounts Department may actually have skills that are better deployed in Marketing or in the Front Office. Making that change may be the best for both the person and the organization.

At times, organizations do not take this kind of step because they are afraid to set precedents for other people who may on a whim wish to change their roles (or for other reasons, such as supervisor conflicts) or for cases in which the organization may not be able to afford to allow even a genuine demand for change. Given the benefits of role change to the person and to the organization when the need is objective, these could be solved by proactively establishing a policy to guide cases of job-person fit and role change.

### Rewarding Work

Enabling and ennobling work conditions are important: this refers to the way jobs are designed so that the person can use all his faculties—intellect and will as well as the body—at work, so that the person does not stagnate. This work is more befitting to a human being since it respects his nature, unlike if the person were doing work that a machine could do. Whenever there is a real need to employ human beings in monotonous, mechanical, and/or repetitive work, it is advisable to design the job as much as possible to allow an element of initiative and innovation in order to engage the intellect and let the person exercise that which makes him human. It is always possible to find a way to find this dimension that allows man to create—perhaps by assigning some other tasks to the person to provide intellectual stimulation. There are many ways of sweeping a room. At the same time, manual work is noble work—the body is essential to human nature.

However, there is work that is demeaning because it goes against or harms human nature. Prostitution fosters the reduction of a human being to a thing, an item that can be paid for. When people are forced into prostitution and have to sell their bodies for a living, this is a sign of a greatly impoverished and dehumanizing society. The same applies to slave trade and to any working conditions that violate human rights. Other instances include workplaces that condone bullying, harassment (sexual or otherwise), stressful work that harms health, excessive intrusiveness of work into personal and family life, unrealistic target setting, etc. Giving people a fair workload and respecting their right to rest—the standard is a certain proportion of hours daily, of days monthly, and of weeks yearly—are important for them to be able to continue to work well.

In a more subtle way, organizations may undermine human dignity and therefore the individual good of their staff and the common good of society with practices that are not blatantly unjust but yet subject people to indignity. This has at times been dubbed workplace incivility. Attention should be paid to this more latent form of injustice in order to root it out wherever necessary.

## Fair Pay

It is very difficult to determine or legislate fair pay. In some economies, small organizations may encounter genuine difficulties in paying a minimum wage and yet they provide employment to people who otherwise would be jobless non-earners. The provision of intangible benefits—such as training and development, flextime, mentoring to another job, etc.—is a way through which actual salaries can be complemented in such cases. Another issue related with workplace ethics is that of child labor. Child labor is wrong because children should not be made to bear responsibilities beyond their stage of human development and should have access to education, play, and other intrinsic goods suitable to their age in order to guarantee them active freedom for a more fulfilling future. However, one must understand situations where the family would starve if the children did not work, and we are all called to do what we can to find solutions to such dilemmas. In addition, child labor must be distinguished from the practice of apprenticeships in which the educational system is predicated precisely on children being taught skills to earn their livelihood in future.[2]

Related to the matter of fair remuneration, it could be also interesting to consider the lack of respect for workplace boundaries of time and space that is on the rise. People are expected to be available all the time instead of only during preagreed working hours, but they gradually become permanently tied to the office and at the beck and call of their bosses. Intrusions into private and family life ensue, causing stress, tension, and conflicts that mar the fulfillment of the person. Yet the persons affected may not even realize the damage they are suffering, they are often so afraid of losing their jobs that they jump to pick every call and give up their time to rest almost cheerfully, to the extent of apologizing for having delayed responding to an email because of being in the shower on a Sunday morning. Unfortunately, there is no remuneration that could compensate for what is being lost—time for oneself, time for family and friends, time for other avenues for development and fulfillment, etc.—since these things are immaterial and cannot be equated to material goods such as a fat bank account or a flashy car or sponsored trips abroad.

## Person-Organization Match

At times, there could be a mismatch between a person and the organization in which he finds himself. This would seem to be a problem of job fit, but at a higher level. In countries where the rate of unemployment is very high, people take whatever job is available—a sensible way to proceed but perhaps not optimal and needing careful management. In a few cases, it just will not work out, as, for example, if a person who finds it impossible to be discreet were to get a job with the FBI. In most cases, it is important to accept the discrepancy and do the best within one's ability so that neither the organization nor the person suffers harm. In fact, if things are well managed, the organization will benefit from a fresh and innovative approach to things and the person will develop new insights and skills. It is possible that after a while, even if there is an opportunity to move to a different, more ideally suited job, the person may prefer to remain where he is because he has already adapted so well. However, in cases where the only reason the person is not moving is inertia, not that he is performing well on the job, etc., it might be good for the organization to actively counsel him out and to help him to move to a new role in a new organization where he will better fit and grow.

In cases where the problem is a clash of values, and attempts to reconcile have failed, perhaps the two parties need to split ways. When the values of an organization are harmful to human nature, then it is even more imperative that the person finds a way to get out of such an environment as soon as possible. Otherwise, he may end up losing his own positive values and adopting almost unconsciously those of the organization.

There are a few instances in which the products or processes of work are contrary to human dignity. This, for example, would be the case of demeaning advertising, the sale of pornography, etc. Such are unethical because they go against the nature of man and reduce him to the level of an animal. They are capitalizing on human degradation and preying on human weaknesses, as would happen with our earlier illustration of a man reduced to the level of a monkey and reacting in the same way as a monkey reacts to a banana. Rather than creating value, such businesses are value destroyers and should have no business existing, *pun intended*.

## Value Congruence

Organizations that set down some corporate values and are serious about them are confronted by the challenge of getting all staff to buy into those values. In the processes of recruitment, training, and rewarding, they need to be clear about the importance of these values. If an organization says that integrity is a corporate value but people observe that it is those who act without integrity that get promoted, they will readjust their understanding of what really is the corporate value of the organization.

At times, organizations simply do not intend to "walk the talk." Someone gets a job in an organization that states its corporate values are integrity, honesty, and customer service and discovers that in fact there is no integrity in the system and the processes are designed to shaft customers. The person may need to find a different job in an organization that better reflects his personal values.

## Workplace Culture and Structuration

As with any other environment, the workplace culture can affect a person and gradually change his values. The converse is also true. A person with a strong enough character and persuasive skills could affect and change the values of the place in which he works. This interactive effect is characteristic of the structuration process in which persons determine culture and culture affects persons. If someone experiences a clash of values within an organization because the organization does not practice what they preach and does not leave quickly, the person may gradually start to lower his own standards in order to fit into his environment and may end up watering down his value system. Thus, it is important to choose well the place where one works in order to put down roots in the right soil where one can truly flourish.

## Coffee Cues

Business owners should understand the nature of human beings who work in the enterprises they set up and do their best to ensure that they provide ennobling work and a good environment that is conducive to human development and fulfillment.

## Exercise

Think of any organization in which you have been employed in the past. Identify things in the environment that promote or inhibit human work physically, psychologically, or mentally/spiritually.

# MODULE 4

# The Full Picture

# CHAPTER 14

# Business in Society

Firms are special persons, with special duties. They are citizens of the society like other persons. All the rest of the society is their potential customers. In law, businesses are legal persons with an existence acknowledged as independent of their promoters. However, they are not persons in every sense of the word. Responsibility can be attributed to them as persons and citizens only when we acknowledge that they are in fact made up of human beings. It is in this sense that we can speak of the need to have ethical or virtuous organizations, knowing that the organization's decisions are extensions of the decisions of the people within and behind it. Indeed, on occasion the veil can be pulled back to reveal who is behind the organization and hold them liable for the actions of the organizations, since it was in order to serve society better that the concept of corporate personality was instituted. Thus, firms exist for society—to serve people—to create value by providing goods and services that are good. It is not always easy to determine what the best decision for society is in specific circumstances, but nevertheless the attempt must be made. Areas of concern about the responsibility of business in society usually revolve around the impact of business activities on society and on the environment, that is, on people and on the planet.

## Case: Cancer in Taranto

Italian steel giant ordered to upgrade but plant kept open by Staff WritersRome (AFP) Aug 7, 2012.

An Italian court Tuesday ordered the country's biggest steel plant to clean up its act but did not call for closure despite fears that chemicals spewed by the unit were behind the high cancer rates in the region.

One of Europe's biggest steel factories, the ILVA plant had become the scene of a fierce stand-off between those who want it closed and thousands of families that depend on it at a time of worsening economic crisis.

The plant is located in the poor southern city of Taranto.

Tuesday's ruling partly reversed a decision by prosecutors in July to shut down the most polluting part of the plant, as the chairman of ILVA said the factory could be kept running while the necessary upgrades are made.

The decision safeguards the jobs of 11,500 workers in the impoverished region. The court also released five of the eight ILVA executives put under house arrest following a health scare investigation.

Environment Minister Corrado Clini, who slammed as "unacceptable to have to choose between bread and poison," said he was confident "the company's efforts and the resources from the government will allow the plant to avoid closure."

Experts had found that chemicals spilling from the plant are behind high cancer rates and cardiovascular and respiratory diseases among workers and locals but the threat to close the plant had sparked protests and angered the country's labor unions.

ILVA chairman Bruno Ferrante, who has been named as the state administrator, will oversee the 336-million-euro ($414 million) cleanup plan funded by the government.

"All the interventions necessary at the ILVA plant can be carried out without interrupting production," Nicola Pirrone, head of the CNR Institute of Atmospheric Pollution Research, said following the court's ruling.

"Turning the chimney stacks off without damaging the plant is a lengthy and costly procedure. It's best that it is avoided. Everything, including installing pollution monitoring systems, can be done with them on," he said.

ILVA, which is owned by the Riva Group, produced nearly 30 percent of Italy's steel output in 2011.

An Italian study last year found that Taranto residents suffered from a "mortality excess" of between 10 percent and 15 percent, due to the release of dioxin and other chemicals causing cancer, respiratory, and cardiovascular diseases.

Environmental association "Taranto Breathes" had hailed the magistrates' initial decision to shut down areas of the plant as "a historic turnaround," praising the courts "for intervening where politics has failed."

But workers backed by Italy's three biggest trade unions had called on the government to protect their jobs, preferring, as one employer told Italian media, "to die of cancer than of hunger."

### Coffee Quiz

1. Should the plant be closed down?
2. Do you know of any businesses with this kind of negative impact?

## Environmental Concerns: Externalities and Free-riding

A free-rider is a person who does not bear the full cost of his actions. Usually, others pay the cost and the free-rider cannot be excluded from enjoying the benefits despite not having contributed positively, or at times having contributed negatively. A good example is that of the tenant who refuses to contribute to hiring a security guard for the estate. If the other tenants put funds together and hire a guard, it is impossible for them to achieve their aim and exclude the defaulter from the enjoyment. Hence, they have no choice but to allow him to enjoy the heightened security and to perhaps think of some other way to sanction him. In some instances, the minority defaulter may be absolutely faultless, especially when what the others have agreed to do is nonessential, as would be the case if the fundraising were for planting flowers around the walls of the estate. He could not be obliged to place any priority on flower planting above other uses he might have for his money. In fact, he might well be allergic to flowers and therefore reasonably object to contributing to their being planted. In the former case, he would still be a free-rider but reasonably so. In the latter case, he would not even be a free-rider at all, since he would not be deriving any enjoyment from the flowers.

We can apply this analogy to businesses that do nothing to preserve the society and environment in which they operate or even carry out actions that are destructive of the environment. They need the society and the environment in order to exist—it would be absurd to think otherwise—but they free-ride on the efforts of the other members of society to benefit themselves. This is not an equitable state of affairs and many people have responded to it by calling for change or acting for change—personal and corporate social responsibility initiatives, social entrepreneurship, impact investing—that would lead to business models that are sustainable because they do not destroy the society and the environment that make up their ecosystem.

Governments also have a role to play in incentivizing businesses to sit up and take their responsibilities seriously. So long as it is possible to get away with free-riding, many companies will continue to do so. They ignore the externalities—the negative impact of their businesses on the environment—and leave the cleaning up of the mess to others in present and future generations. By doing so, they do not bear the full cost of the business they do, but they rake in the profits. If, for example, they could be required to always deduct the cost of their impact on the environment and on people (it would not be easy but let us suppose it could be done) from their profits and return the amount to government at the end of each financial year, they would surely be more careful of their business activities and would have an incentive to innovate to find less harmful ways to make profit. Also, bearing their full cost would create a more level playing field between the companies that try to be responsible corporate citizens and those that do not, and therefore make being good more attractive to those who already wish it as well as making it easier for them to do well by doing good.

## Personal and Corporate Social Responsibility

In some cases, business leaders individually find ways to contribute to society and encourage others within their organization to do so. For example, in Chevron Nigeria Ltd., staff are encouraged to give some hours volunteering as teachers in a nearby school where the students do not have access to a high quality of education. The example of a CEO establishing an NGO in order to contribute to building up society is likely to encourage others within the same firm to do something, no matter how small, in the same line. There are also corporate social responsibility efforts—where the company as an entity carries out some activities that portray good citizenship behavior. It has happened at times that corporate social responsibility actions have been actually marketing gimmicks—to make consumers happy—and not really because the company espouses the principles behind them; however, in such cases other actions of the company may reveal the double-dealing and the company may suffer a severe backlash.[1] One of the good signs to know whether a company is sincere in its corporate social responsibility statements is to look into how it treats its employees. An organization that treats its people badly cannot be said to be socially responsible. In sum, it is important for companies to go beyond slogans and branding efforts and actually make a difference around them.

## Social Entrepreneurship and Impact Investing

Entrepreneurs who see a social need and try to fulfill it while making a profit or at least sustaining themselves are called social entrepreneurs. This idea of doing business primarily in response to a social need has widened of late to include non-entrepreneurs who invest in socially impacting businesses, and it is known as impact investing. In the latter case, these businesses deliberately choose a business model to make money while addressing some societal ill. A good example is TOMS Shoes. The founder CEO started his business to provide shoes for children in Argentina who had none. Each of his customers is offered the opportunity to pay for two pairs of shoes—one for himself and one for a child in Argentina. It has attracted many people who identify with his vision and therefore buy TOMS shoes and market it to others.

## Sustainable Business Models

Many other concepts and initiatives continue to come up in order to develop more sustainable business models—triple bottom line accounting[2], market inclusion[3], responsible financing, etc.—and more ways to measure ethical and responsible business—carbon credits, social stock exchange, social GDP, etc. Disenfranchised people are a threat to the rest of society—for example, some of the people affected by the Niger Delta fracas in Nigeria have reacted by taking up arms and terrorist activities, having lost their means of livelihood due to the destruction of arable land in their home villages. There is no Planet B, and so it is important to safeguard the one we have. Business will last only so long as there are still customers and there is still a planet to exist on.

## Coffee Cues

When there seems to be a choice between the devil and the deep blue sea, it is useful to remember that perhaps there are other alternatives to explore. It is not always that one has only two choices to select from. Think outside the box. What else could the company do? How else could they manage the situation?

## Projects

In small groups of 6 to 10, work for 4 weeks to develop the blueprint for a student-led-activity that will have a social dimension. At the end of each week, each group should make a presentation of their progress so far to the whole class. The class will give feedback on each presentation and make suggestions that could improve the work. The final presentation will be assessed based on relevance, creativity and originality, practicability, compatibility with schoolwork, projected social impact, and quality of work done.

Each student should make a personal social responsibility (PSR) plan—it could involve greater respect for people, for the society, or for the environment. It should have realistic and measurable action points. At the end of the course, a report of the progress with the PSR plan should be submitted and assessed based on how the challenges encountered so far in carrying out the plan have been overcome.

# CHAPTER 15

# In Conclusion

In all chapters, we have tried to understand better the makeup of a human being. We can never fully do so, but at least we have made a useful attempt, which is helping us to lay good foundations for treating people ethically and managing organizations sustainably. Both require the deepened insight into human nature that we now have—one that enables a clear line of sight for linking individual actions and corporate behavior to personal and corporate responsibility to society and to future generations.

Responsible management is that which keeps in view all stakeholders and truly creates lasting value for the present and the future. Value thus created is multidimensional and not simply valuable in one dimension and harmful in others, or valuable now and harmful later.

## Case: T and K Chalk

Hello,

I am ADELAJA BOLUTIFE an MBA student of class 1.

I want to thank you for the eye-opening exposure you made me have with your lectures. For me, the best moments were those days when we had industry players coming around to share their views.

And, I have made moves to be more ethical in my dealings. There is one I am proud to reveal. I am a producer of chalks. I trade under the name of T and K Chalk. Sure, I enforce quality but I must admit that I directed my staffs to pack up broken pieces alongside the good ones into the carton—surreptitiously.

Your classes were "aha" events for me.

I had to redirect my people to stop the practice henceforth and I actually "bulk SMS-ed" my customers about it too. I offered to send them small extra packs to serve as palliatives. My sales staff said the customers called in and were impressed with the owning up.

Surprisingly, one of my sales guys said someone sent him a text offering to buy the broken ones henceforth. And a proprietor's husband sent a text that he would be coming to the company this weekend to strengthen our knowledge about the production of chalk, in a bid to reduce or eradicate wastage. He would undertake to do this free of charge. Why? He said what we did resonates with his religious views.

All this because I was in your lectures.

In addition, I will work more on those areas that need correction—personally—now.

Thank you for the insights. My Deeper Life-enthusiast mum couldn't do it.

Thank you for making me see the VALUE in being ethical. Thanks.

Maximum respects,

Bolutife.

## Coffee Quiz

1. Advise Bolutife on how to ensure the long-term sustainability of the choices he is making.
2. What other ways are there to innovate and so create additional value?
3. How else could they lower their costs?
4. Would your recommendations be the same if this was a professional services outfit or a multinational manufacturing firm?

## Taking Concrete and Practical Steps

In the 2012 Olympics, a swimmer won the gold medal in the breaststroke event. After being awarded the medal, he admitted that he won because he did extra dolphin strokes in the middle of the race. His excuse was that others do the same and he wanted to win. Asking her readers if it makes sense to cheat because others do it, Katie Hinderer of *Tiger Print* frames the question: "Do we admire integrity or the medal?"[1] In the final analysis, each person has to make a decision as to the kind of human being he wishes to be. Knowledge is only a beginning; willingness is critical in order to go ahead. Determination relies on constant openness to knowing and repeated application of willing in order to make progress.

It is not enough to see clearly what needs to be done. One also requires moral courage, expressed in will power, to do it. Will power is built up gradually, not waiting for the moment in which there are very tough decisions. Having come to the end of this book/course and understood a little bit better the nature of human beings, it would be really useful to specify some concrete and practical steps to take in order to be a better person and to manage people around you better. Start with little things. This is the key to being able to take the right decision and follow through with it later on if and when the need arises.

### Coffee Cues

Despite its not being the easiest option, the choice of acting ethically is the more sustainable one. Perhaps this is why some firms actually regard ethical behavior as part of a risk-management strategy. T and K Chalks could have continued business as usual and they would be exposed to the risk of either the consumers getting wise to what was going on or the regulators catching up with them. However, even if no external traps tripped them up, the consciousness of the harm they were doing to others would have continued eating at them and marring their capacity for fulfillment as human beings. Man is to the very end a social being and when he harms others, he harms himself even more.

# Notes

## Chapter 1

1. *The New Oxford Dictionary of English* (1998), p. 71.
2. *The New Oxford Dictionary of English* (1998), p. 893.
3. *The New Oxford Dictionary of English* (1998), p. 892. In the Longman's Dictionary of Contemporary English, a human (being) is a man, woman or child, not an animal.
4. *The New Oxford Dictionary of English* (1998), p. 1384.
5. Boethius (1343D) cf. Saranyana (1996).
6. http://www.na-businesspress.com/ijbaopen.html. Retrieved October 18, 2012.
7. Baba (2006), pp. 83–117.
8. *Ibid*. See also Jordan (2002).
9. *Ibid*.
10. Mele and Dierksmeier (2012).
11. Zaleznik (2004), p. 126.
12. *The New Oxford Dictionary of English* (1998), p. 893.
13. Hartman and DesJardins (2011).
14. "Good" here means ontological good and not moral good; the latter is applicable only to beings who are free and can choose.

## Chapter 2

1. We normally use definitions to delimit; for example, a bird is a feathered biped, usually to show that it is different from biped mammals (for example, lemurs, kangaroos, and humans), which are not feathered.
2. *Nichomachean Ethics*, 1.13.
3. Knowledge that he detects through the five senses of hearing, smell, sight, touch, and taste.
4. Non-sensible because they cannot be detected by the five senses.
5. "Spiritual" or "immaterial" means having no parts and therefore being indestructible.
6. A town in Nigeria.
7. Airlines usually warn, implicitly appealing to reason, that this instinct should not be followed: the mother should put on her own mask first before attempting to put on the infant's.

8. *The New Oxford Dictionary of English*, p. 959.
9. The body is not a block of wood. It has to be taken care of.
10. Abraham Maslow (1954).

# Chapter 3

1. Reichmann (1985).
2. Von Hildebrand (2011).

# Chapter 4

1. Such as mathematical concepts that do not exist in reality, for example, one has never met an actual triangle.
2. Unicorns, griffins, merfolk, and suchlike.
3. Directed by Phyllida Lloyd and produced by Damian Jones, it was first released on 26th December 2011, in Australia.
4. One reason for this, while not being among the most important, is that it in fact corresponds better to our nature as rational animals.

# Chapter 5

1. *Nicomachean Ethics*.
2. Cf. Thomas Aquinas, *Summa Theologiae*, II-II, q.148, a. 3. John Paul II *The Splendor of Truth* (Veritatis Splendor). No. 72 Encyclical letter 1993.
3. Different from the love mentioned in Chapter 3 which is at the level of passion and therefore transient.
4. Rotter's instrument can be found at http://www.psych.uncc.edu/pagoolka /LocusofControl-intro.html, last accessed on 29th September 2012.

# Chapter 6

1. In Chapter 5; Note that, for those raising a family, using operant conditioning could initially help to shape the behavior of children when one carefully selects what kind of behavior to reinforce. However, as the children grow and their intellectual capacity increases, appeal to reason should increase so that the children can exercise their freedom by choosing.
2. Released on 17th March, 2004 and directed by Christophe Barratier.
3. At the Lagos Business School, Pan-African University, Lagos, Nigeria.
4. Pratchett (2002).

5. Holm (2004).
6. Act with the use of reason.
7. As opposed to reviewing the past to learn from it for personal gain and to positively impact others.
8. A mental habit akin to directing vehicle traffic without being caught up in it.

# Chapter 7

1. Two areas of the city linked by a bridge; it would take one and a half hours on the average to drive from home to work.
2. A suburb of the city.
3. Produced and directed by Jennifer Arnold and released on 12th July 2010, this film was an Emmy Award nominee for "Best Documentary" in 2011 and also won the Humanitas Prize for Documentary in 2010; more information at http://asmallact.com/

# Chapter 8

1. Though such stories often lack scientific rigor, they show that feral children do not develop properly as humans due to having been raised by animals.
2. Extremes are always fraught with danger.
3. The Burning Train, produced by B.R. Films and United Producers and released on 20th March 1980.
4. McGue and Bouchard (1998).
5. Referring here only to their genetic similarities and not to the nature of human beings in general.

# Chapter 9

1. Hartman and DesJardins (2011).
2. An essential difference is what sets man apart from animals. Accidental differences do not pertain to the essence, therefore a man continues to be a man and to claim all his basic human rights irrespective of whether he has a limo and a penthouse or an uncle on the board of directors or two eyes, or is HIV positive.
3. Pratchett (2002).

# Chapter 10

1. There is no intention to imply (here or anywhere else in this book) that NGOs are always "good" places to work or that Chen could not have found

a bank or multinational with the same enabling environment he found in
the NGO. The narrative is simply presented as the factual story that it is.

2. Goals that do not harm others or ourselves.

3. Finnis (2011).

## Chapter 11

1. Carson (2004).

2. Holm (2004).

3. Culpable ignorance, however, may not remove responsibility; for example,
   directors of a business who neglect their oversight duties cannot claim that
   they did not know what was going on in a fraudulent company.

4. Frankl (2006).

## Chapter 12

1. The more of the truth one has, the clearer the good is, and the freer the
   person is to act.

2. Prudence comes first because it is ruled by the intellect; the other three are
   ruled by the will and the will follows the intellect, as already mentioned
   earlier.

3. His goodness and benevolence turn out to be self-love in disguise.

## Chapter 13

1. Hall and Chandler (2005).

2. The Spook's apprentice could hardly be described as a child laborer.

## Chapter 14

1. As happened when the "greenwashing" of British Petroleum was exposed.

2. Including nonfinancial indices (social and environmental indices).

3. Working toward access to markets for everyone without discrimination.

## Chapter 15

1. Do we admire integrity or the medal? by Katie Hinderer, 20 Aug 2012,
   available at http://www.mercatornet.com/tiger_print/view/11132, last
   viewed on 18 Oct 2012.

# References

Aquinas, T. *Summa theologiae.* II-II, q.148, a. 3.

Aristotle (1925). *The Nicomachean ethics.* Oxford – New York: Oxford University Press.

Arjoon, S. (2007). Ethical decision-making: A case for the triple font-theory. *Journal of Business Ethics 71*(4), 395–410.

Baba, M. (2006). Anthropology and business. In H. James Birx, (Ed.), *Encyclopedia of anthropology.* Thousand Oaks, CA: Sage Publications.

Boethius, S. *Liber de persona et duabus naturis contra Eutychen et Nestorium.* Chapter III, PL 64, 133754, ed. and tr. by Stewart, H. F, Rand, E. K. & Tester, S. J. (1973) in *The theological tractates and the consolation of philosophy* (pp. 76–126), Cambridge, MA: Harvard University Press.

Carson, B. (2004). *Gifted hands* (New edition). United States: Zondervan.

De Caussade, J. P. (2010). *The sacrament of the present moment* (Reissue edition). San Francisco, CA: Harper. Also available: (Ed. J. Ramiere) from CreateSpace Independent Publishing Platform.

Finnis, J. (2011). *Natural law and natural rights* (2nd ed.) United States: Oxford University Press.

Frankl, V. E. (2006). *Man's search for meaning.* Boston, MA: Beacon Press.

Goleman, D. (1995). *Emotional intelligence.* New York, NY: Bantam Books.

Goleman, D. (1998). *Working with emotional intelligence.* New York, NY: Bantam Books.

Hall, D. T. and Chandler, D. E. (2005). Psychological success: When the career is a calling, *Journal of Organizational Behaviour 26*(2), 155–176.

Hartman, L. P. and DesJardins, J. (2011). *Business ethics: Decision making for personal integrity and social responsibility* (2nd ed.). New York, NY: McGraw Hill/Irwin.

Hinderer, K. (2012). *Do we admire integrity or the medal?* Available at http://www.mercatornet.com/tiger_print/view/11132

Holm, A. (2004) *I am David.* Orlando, FL: Harcourt Children's Books.

John Paul II (1993). The splendor of truth (Veritatis splendor), Rome: Libreria Editrice Vaticana, available at http://www.vatican.va/holy_father/john_paul_ii/encyclicals/documents/hf_jp-ii_enc_06081993_veritatis-splendor_en.html.

Jordan, A. T. (2002). *Business anthropology.* Prospect Heights Waveland Press

Maslow, A. (1954). *Motivation and personality* (3rd ed.). New York, NY: Harper and Row Publishers.

McGue, M. and Bouchard, T. J., Jr. (1998). Genetic and environmental influences on human behavioral differences. *Annual Review Neurosci 21*, 1–24.

Mele, D. and Dierksmeier, C. (Eds.). (2012). *Human development in business.* Houndmills: Palgrave Macmillan.

Ogunyemi, A. (2012a). A social entrepreneurship model from Nigeria. *ACRN Journal of Entrepreneurship Perspectives 1*(1), 137–148.

Ogunyemi, A. (2012b). Workforce diversity at the Lagos Business School, Pan-African University, Nigeria. In Chaunda L. Scott and Marilyn Y. Byrd (Eds.), *Handbook of research on workforce diversity in a global society: Technologies and concepts* (pp. 73–87). USA (Hershey, PA): IGI Global (doi:10.4018/978-1 -4666-1812-1).

Pratchett, T. (2002). *Thief of time* (New edition). UK: Corgi.

Reichmann, J. B. (1985). *Philosophy of the human person.* Chicago Loyola University Press.

Saranyana, J. (1996). *History of medieval philosophy.* Manila: Sinag-Tala Publishers.

*The New Oxford Dictionary of English.* (1998). United States: Oxford University Press.

Von Hildebrand, A. (2011). *In defense of feelings.* Available at http://www. holyspiritinteractive.org/library/718#.UIB-p8XR6Ok

Zaleznik, A. (72004). Managers and leaders: Are they different? *Harvard Business Review 82*(1), 74–81.

# Index

## OTHER TITLES IN OUR PRINCIPLES FOR RESPONSIBLE MANAGEMENT EDUCATION (PRME) COLLECTION

Oliver Laasch, Monterrey Institute of Technology, Collection Editor

- *Business Integrity in Practice: Insights from International Case Studies* by Agata Stachowicz-Stanusch
- *Academic Ethos Management Building the Foundation for Integrity in Management Education* by Agata Stachowicz-Stanusch
- *Marketing to the Low-Income Consumer* by Paulo Cesar Motta
- *Educating for Values-Driven Leadership: Giving Voice to Values* by Mary Gentile
- *Fostering Spirituality in the Workplace: A Leader's Guide to a Sustainable Business Environment* by Priscilla Berry
- *Managing Corporate Responsibility in Emerging Markets: Issues, Cases, and Solutions* by Jenik Radon

---

## Announcing the Business Expert Press Digital Library

*Concise E-books Business Students Need for Classroom and Research*

This book can also be purchased in an e-book collection by your library as
- a one-time purchase,
- that is owned forever,
- allows for simultaneous readers,
- has no restrictions on printing, and
- can be downloaded as PDFs from within the library community.

Our digital library collections are a great solution to beat the rising cost of textbooks. e-books can be loaded into their course management systems or onto student's e-book readers.

The **Business Expert Press** digital libraries are very affordable, with no obligation to buy in future years. For more information, please visit **www.businessexpertpress.com/librarians**. To set up a trial in the United States, please contact **Adam Chesler** at *adam.chesler@businessexpertpress .com* for all other regions, contact **Nicole Lee** at *nicole.lee@igroupnet.com*.

9 781606 495049